YESTERDAY'S VOICES ON THE INNER LIFE

A Prose and Poetry Anthology

Compiled by A. A. Willis

LUMINARE PRESS

WWW.LUMINAREPRESS.COM

Cover Design: Melissa K. Thomas

Luminare Press
442 Charnelton
Eugene, OR 97401
www.luminarepress.com

LCCN: 2019910575
ISBN: 978-1-64388-168-3

*"To all who feel wonder and awe for the universe,
who practice care and sustainability for our world, and
who feel kindness and compassion for others"*

TABLE OF CONTENTS

Part One
ON MIND, THOUGHT, THE INNER LIFE

Part Two
ON THE NATURE OF THINGS

Part Three

ON CHARACTER,
CONDUCT, VIRTUES

INTRODUCTION

⸺⸙⸺

A CONSTANT THROUGHOUT HISTORY HAS BEEN humanity's quest in its collective search for purpose, happiness, and inner peace for the individual. The verse and prose selections presented in this collection are drawn from a wide variety of world literature of the past that targets these basic desires that have been sought after over the millennia.

In today's fast-paced and sometimes chaotic world, identifying and utilizing resources that can help a person simplify, slow down, and reflect on the inner life is more important than ever, no matter your life situation. Words of yesterday's sages, poets, and thinkers have always filled this need and have stood the test of time down through the centuries to bring their wisdom to our present day. The selections offered here give some examples of the great and small truths that can be found in prose and poetry of the past in the world's wide range of literature. To visit these earlier sources and there discover their words on simplicity, inner peace, life purpose, moderation, and other wisdom can deepen and broaden awareness for the important aspects of life.

Since antiquity, the words of prophets, philosophers, mystics, clerics, sages, and poets have given our world this vast treasure of literature to inspire, educate, and guide us on our journey. Time-tested and time-honored thoughts of men and women thinkers from the past are still very relevant today and can supply proven guidance in the conduct of life. They exhort us to reflect on how we see our world, others, ourselves, and how best to live. Universal principles and perspectives written about down through history can guide us on this path of discovery. They can help us transcend the conditioned existence of today's modern society with its unbalanced emphasis on money, power, celebrity, possessions, status, instant gratification, and social divisions.

From the essays of Emerson, to the poems of Shakespeare and Longfellow, to the meditations and letters of the Stoics, to the songs of Kabir, and to the prose poetry of the Bible, the Tao Te Ching, the Bhagavad Gita, and the Dhammapada, this eclectic compilation tries to supply just a small taste of the world literature of yesterday that may offer guides to reflection and glimpses of the underlying Reality to the new or experienced seeker. In epic, essay, treatise, play, poem, and prayer, the timeless messages from well-known and lesser known voices continue to speak to us in these modern times.

Poets have always had a prominent place in literature for the mind throughout history, and poetry has been called the "language of the heart." This collection uses a wide variety of poetic selections on these perspectives to complement the prose offerings on these universal concerns.

*"The poets are they who see that spiritual is greater
than any material force, that thoughts rule the world."*

—RALPH WALDO EMERSON.
Parnassus. An Anthology of Poetry.

The unifying theme throughout this collection is that we
are one with the universe, nature, and with each other.
The broad spectrum of literature sources from the past
embodies these timeless truths of unity, oneness, and inter-
connections in all their forms. The various selections have
been subjectively grouped into three broad categories
– mind and thought, the nature of things, character and
conduct. This collection has sections and chapters but can
be opened at any point to read inspirational viewpoints and
insights on the nature of things.

The ever-increasing pace of today's world and the
expanding multiplicity of things that vie for our attention
all combine to make the inner journey more difficult. For
those on or beginning this path, visiting relevant literature
of the past can support their efforts in that endeavor.

*"As the soul is dyed by the thoughts, let no day pass
without contact with the best literature of the world."*

—SIR WILLIAM OSLER.
A Way of Life

Part One

ON MIND, THOUGHT, THE INNER LIFE

For as he thinketh in his heart, so is he.

—PROVERBS 23:7. *KJV.*

The aphorism, "As a man thinketh in his heart so is he," not only embraces the whole of a man's being but is so comprehensive as to reach out to every condition and circumstance of his life. A man is literally what he thinks, his character being the complete sum of all his thoughts.

—JAMES ALLEN.
As A Man Thinketh.

Such as are thy habitual thoughts, such also will be the character of thy mind, for the soul is dyed by the thoughts.

—MARCUS AURELIUS.
The Meditations of Marcus Aurelius.

Words and thoughts are a tremendous vibratory force, ever molding man's body and affairs.

—FLORENCE S. Shinn.
The Game of Life and How to Play It.

The world is such stuff as ideas are made of. Thought possesses all things. But the world is not unreal. It extends infinitely beyond our private consciousness, because it is the world of a universal mind.

—JOSIAH ROYCE.
The Spirit of Modern Philosophy;
An Essay in the Form of Lectures.

And be not conformed to this world: but be ye transformed by the renewing of your mind.

—ROMANS 12:2. *KJV.*

I hold it true that thoughts are things;
They're endowed with bodies and breath and wings;
And that we send them forth to fill
The world with good results, or ill.
That which we call our secret thought
Speeds forth to earth's remotest spot,
Leaving its blessings or its woes
Like tracks behind it as it goes.
We build our future, thought by thought,
For good or ill, yet know it not.
Yet, so the universe was wrought.
Thought is another name for fate;
Choose, then, thy destiny and wait.
For love brings love and hate brings hate.

—HENRY VAN DYKE.
"Thoughts Are Things."

As with events, so is it with thoughts. When I watch that flowing river, which, out of regions I see not, pours for a season its streams into me, I see that I am a pensioner; not a cause, but a surprised spectator of this ethereal water; that I desire and look up and put myself in the attitude of reception, but from some alien energy the visions come.

—RALPH WALDO EMERSON.
"The Over-Soul." *Essays, First Series.*

Mind is the Master—power that molds and makes,
And Man is Mind, and ever more he takes
The Tool of Thought, and shaping what he wills,
Brings forth a thousand joys, a thousand ills—
He thinks in secret and it comes to pass;
Environment is but his looking-glass.

—JAMES ALLEN.
As A Man Thinketh.

There is one mind common to all individual men. Every man is an inlet to the same and to all of the same. He that is once admitted to the right of reason is made a freeman of the whole estate. What Plato has thought, he may think; what a saint has felt, he may feel; what at any time has befallen any man, he can understand. Who hath access to this universal mind is a party to all that is or can be done, for this is the only and sovereign agent.

—RALPH WALDO EMERSON.
"History." *Essays, First Series.*

As the soul is dyed by the thoughts, let no day pass without contact with the best literature of the world.

—SIR WILLIAM OSLER.
A Way of Life.

Which of us feels, or knows, that he wants peace?

There are two ways of getting it, if you do want it. The first is wholly in your own power; to make yourselves nests of pleasant thoughts. Those are nests on the sea indeed, but safe beyond all others; only they need much art in the building. None of us yet know, for none of us have been taught in early youth, what fairy palaces we may build of beautiful thought—proof against all adversity. Bright fancies, satisfied memories, noble histories, faithful sayings, treasure-houses of precious and restful thoughts, which care cannot disturb, nor pain make gloomy, nor poverty take away from us—houses built without hands, for our souls to live in.

—JOHN RUSKIN.
"The Eagle's Nest." *The Works of John Ruskin.*

Every thought you entertain is a force that goes out, and every thought comes back laden with its kind. This is an immutable law. Every thought you entertain has moreover a direct effect upon your body. Love and its kindred emotions are the normal and the natural, those in accordance with the eternal order of the universe, for "God is love." These have a life-giving, health-engendering influence upon your body, besides beautifying your countenance, enriching your voice, and making you ever more attractive in every way. And as it is true that in the degree that you hold thoughts of love for all, you call the same from them in return, and as these have a direct effect upon your mind, and through your mind upon your body, it is as so much life force added to your own from without. You are then continually building this into both your mental and your physical life, and so your life is enriched by its influence.

—RALPH WALDO TRINE.
In Tune with the Infinite.

Thought is existence. More than that, so far as we are concerned, existence is thought, all our conceptions of existence being some kind or other of thought.

—THOMAS HENRY HUXLEY.
Aphorisms and Reflections.

Be sure that you have made no small progress in the spiritual life, when you can control your imagination, so as to fix it on the duty and occupation actually existing, to the exclusion of the crowd of thoughts which are perpetually sweeping across the mind.

—PERE JEAN NICOLAS GROU.
"Detachment." *The Hidden Life of the Soul.*

The control of the thinking machine is perfectly possible. And since nothing whatever happens to us outside our own brain; since nothing hurts us or gives us pleasure except within the brain, the supreme importance of being able to control what goes on in that mysterious brain is patent. This idea is one of the oldest platitudes, but it is a platitude whose profound truth and urgency most people live and die without realising. People complain of the lack of power to concentrate, not witting that they may acquire the power, if they choose.

—ARNOLD BENNETT.
How to Live on Twenty-four Hours a Day.

What is more easy and sweet than meditation? Yet in this hath God commended His Love, that by meditation it is enjoyed. As nothing is easier than to think, so nothing is more difficult than to think well. The easiness of thinking we received from God, the difficulty of thinking well proceeded from ourselves. Yet in truth, it is far easier to think well than ill, because good thoughts be sweet and delightful: Evil thoughts are full of discontent and trouble. So that an evil habit and custom have made it difficult to think well, not Nature. For by nature nothing is so difficult as to think amiss.

—THOMAS TRAHERNE.
Centuries of Meditations.

Thought is the unconscious and unceasing language of the mind.

—James Lendall Basford.
Sparks from the Philosopher's Stone.

How happy is he born or taught,
That serveth not anothers will;
Whose armour is his honest thought,
And simple truth his highest skill.

—Sir Henry Wotton.
"The Character of a Happy Life." *Reliquiæ Wottonianæ.*

It is good to tame the mind, which is difficult to hold in and flighty, rushing wherever it listeth; a tamed mind brings happiness.

Let the wise man guard his thoughts, for they are difficult to perceive, very artful, and they rush wherever they list: thoughts well guarded bring happiness.

—The Dhammapada.

That Self is indeed Brahman, consisting of knowledge, mind, life, sight, hearing, earth, water, wind, ether, light and no light, desire and no desire, anger and no anger, right or wrong, and all things. Now as a man is like this or like that, according as he acts and according as he behaves, so will he be: - a man of good acts will become good, a man of bad acts, bad. He becomes pure by pure deeds, bad by bad deeds.

And here they say that a person consists of desires. And as is his desire, so is his will; and as is his will, so is his deed; and whatever deed he does, that he will reap.

—"Brihadâranyaka Upanishad IV.4.5."

Thought is deeper than all speech,
Feeling deeper than all thought:
Souls to souls can never teach
What unto themselves was taught.

Only when the Sun of Love
Melts the scattered stars of thought;
Only when we live above
What the dim-eyed world hath taught,

Only when our souls are fed
By the Fount which gave them birth,
And by inspiration led,
Which they never drew from earth,

We, like parted drops of rain,
Swelling till they meet and run,
Shall be all absorbed again,
Melting, flowing into one.

—Christopher Pearse Cranch.
"Gnosis." *Gems of Genius in Poetry and Art.*

Finally, brethren, whatsoever things are true, whatsoever things are honest, whatsoever things are just, whatsoever things are pure, whatsoever things are lovely, whatsoever things are of good report; if there be any virtue, and if there be any praise, think on these things.

—PHILIPPIANS 4:8. *KJV.*

Chapter 2

ON THE INNER JOURNEY, THE SPIRITUAL PATH, THE SPIRITUAL QUEST

O servant, where dost thou seek Me?
Lo! I am beside thee.
I am neither in temple nor in mosque: I am neither in
Kaaba nor in Kailash:
Neither am I in rites and ceremonies, nor in Yoga and
renunciation.
If thou art a true seeker, thou shalt at once see Me: thou shalt
meet Me in a moment of time.
Kabîr says, "O Sadhu! God is the breath of all breath."

—KABIR.
Songs of Kabir.

But seek ye first the kingdom of God, and his righteousness; and all these things shall be added unto you.

—MATTHEW 6:33. *KJV.*

First of all, condemn the life thou art now leading: but when thou hast condemned it, do not despair of thyself—be not like them of mean spirit, who once they have yielded, abandon themselves entirely and as it were allow the torrent to sweep them away. No; learn what the wrestling masters do. Has the boy fallen? "Rise," they say, "wrestle again, till thy strength come to thee." Even thus should it be with thee. For know that there is nothing more tractable than the human soul. It needs but to will, and the thing is done; the soul is set upon the right path: as on the contrary it needs but to nod over the task, and all is lost. For ruin and recovery alike are from within.

—*THE GOLDEN SAYINGS OF EPICTETUS.*

Neither shall they say, Lo here! or, lo there! for, behold, the kingdom of God is within you.

—LUKE 17:21. *KJV.*

I do not ring the temple bell:
I do not set the idol on its throne:
I do not worship the image with flowers.
It is not the austerities that mortify the flesh which are
pleasing to the Lord,
When you leave off your clothes and kill your senses, you
do not please the Lord:
The man who is kind and who practises righteousness,
who remains passive amidst the affairs of the world, who
considers all creatures on earth as his own self,

He attains the Immortal Being, the true God is ever
with him.
Kabîr says: "He attains the true Name whose words are
pure, and who is free from pride and conceit."

—KABIR.
Songs of Kabir.

Thanks for the heavenly message brought by thee,
Child of the wandering sea,
Cast from her lap, forlorn!
From thy dead lips a clearer note is born
Than ever Triton blew from wreathèd horn!
While on mine ear it rings,
Through the deep caves of thought I hear a voice that sings:—
Build thee more stately mansions, O my soul,
As the swift seasons roll!
Leave thy low-vaulted past!
Let each new temple, nobler than the last,
Shut thee from heaven with a dome more vast,
Till thou at length art free,
Leaving thine outgrown shell by life's unresting sea!

—OLIVER WENDELL HOLMES, SR.
"The Chambered Nautilus."

Thus the occupations and businesses of the world have become more and more complicated and troublesome, chiefly owing to the fact that men have forgotten that their real necessities are only three—clothing, food, and shelter, and that these exist only with the object of making the body a fit vehicle for the soul in its journey towards the next world.

—MOHAMMED AL-GHAZZALI.
The Alchemy of Happiness.

Devoted—with a heart grown pure, restrained
In lordly self-control, forgoing wiles
Of song and senses, freed from love and hate,
Dwelling 'mid solitudes, in diet spare,
With body, speech, and will tamed to obey,
Ever to holy meditation vowed,
From passions liberate, quit of the Self,
Of arrogance, impatience, anger, pride;
Freed from surroundings, quiet, lacking nought—
Such an one grows to oneness with the BRAHM.

—THE BHAGAVAD-GITA.

Fortitude, forbearance, self-restraint, no desire for other's wealth, purity, control over the senses, conscious intelligence, spiritual culture, truthfulness, absence of anger, - these ten make up the characteristics of all true religion whatever.

—MANU.
The Spirit of the Upanishads.

Enter the Path! There is no grief like Hate!
No pains like passions, no deceit like sense!
Enter the Path! far hath he gone whose foot
Treads down one fond offence.

Enter the Path! There spring the healing streams
Quenching all thirst! there bloom th' immortal flowers
Carpeting all the way with joy! there throng,
Swiftest and sweetest hours

—EDWIN ARNOLD.
The Light of Asia: Or, The Great Renunciation.

Krishna.
Fearlessness, singleness of soul, the will
Always to strive for wisdom; opened hand
And governed appetites; and piety,
And love of lonely study; humbleness,
Uprightness, heed to injure nought which lives,
Truthfulness, slowness unto wrath, a mind
That lightly letteth go what others prize;
And equanimity, and charity
Which spieth no man's faults; and tenderness
Towards all that suffer; a contented heart,
Fluttered by no desires; a bearing mild,
Modest, and grave, with manhood nobly mixed,
With patience, fortitude, and purity;
An unrevengeful spirit, never given
To rate itself too high;—such be the signs,
O Indian Prince! of him whose feet are set
On that fair path which leads to heavenly birth!

—THE BHAGAVAD-GITA.

Chapter 3

ON PHILOSOPHY

It is the bounty of nature that we live; but of philosophy that we live well, which is in truth a greater benefit than life itself. Not but that philosophy is also the gift of Heaven, so far as to the faculty, but not to the science; for that must be the business of industry. No man is born wise; but wisdom and virtue require a tutor, though we can easily learn to be vicious without a master.

It is philosophy that gives us a veneration for God, a charity for our neighbor, that teaches us our duty to Heaven, and exhorts us to an agreement one with another; it unmasks things that are terrible to us, assuages our lusts, refutes our errors, restrains our luxury, reproves our avarice, and works strangely upon tender natures.

—LUCIUS ANNAEUS SENECA.
"Of A Happy Life." *Seneca's Morals by Way of Abstract.*

And thou shalt know how true is the saying of Cleanthes, that though the words of philosophy may run counter to the opinions of the world, yet have they reason on their side.

—*THE GOLDEN SAYINGS OF EPICTETUS.*

And we must practice what we preach: for philosophy is not a subject for popular ostentation; nor does it rest in words, but in things. It is not an entertainment taken up for delight, or to give a taste to our leisure; but it fashions the mind, governs our actions, tells us what we are to do, and what not. It sits at the helm, and guides us through all hazards: nay, we cannot be safe without it, for every hour gives us occasion to make use of it. It informs us in all the duties of life, piety to our parents, faith to our friends, charity to the miserable, judgment in counsel; it gives us peace by fearing nothing, and riches by coveting nothing.

—Lucius Annaeus Seneca.
"Of A Happy Life." *Seneca's Morals by Way of Abstract.*

Half of ignorance is destroyed by free exchange of thought; half of the remainder is dispelled by application to philosophy; the rest fades away in the light of Self-reflection.

—Yoga Vasishtha.
*The Spirit of the Upanishads
(or the Aphorisms of the Wise).*

Our life is a warfare, and a mere pilgrimage. Fame after life is no better than oblivion. What is it then that will adhere and follow? Only one thing, philosophy. And philosophy doth consist in this, for a man to preserve that spirit which is within him, from all manner of contumelies and injuries, and above all pains or pleasures; never to do anything either rashly, or feignedly, or hypocritically: wholly to depend from himself and his own proper actions: all things that happen unto him to embrace contentedly, as coming from Him from whom he himself also came; and above all things, with all meekness and a calm cheerfulness, to expect death, as being nothing else but the resolution of those elements, of which every creature is composed. And if the elements themselves suffer nothing by this their perpetual conversion of one into another, that dissolution, and alteration, which is so common unto all, why should it be feared by any? Is not this according to nature?

—MARCUS AURELIUS.
The Meditations of Marcus Aurelius.

Philosophers are not only those that contemplate happiness, but practise virtue. He is a Philosopher that subdues his vices, lives by reason, orders his desires, rules his passions, and submits not to his senses, nor is guided by the customs of this world. He despiseth those riches which men esteem, he despiseth those honours which men esteem, he forsaketh those pleasures which men esteem. And having proposed to himself a superior end than is commonly discerned, bears all discouragements, breaks through all difficulties and lives unto it: that having seen the secrets and the secret beauties of the highest reason, orders his conversation, and lives by rule: though in this age it be held never so strange that he should do so.

—THOMAS TRAHERNE.
Centuries of Meditations.

Of all men they alone are at leisure who take time for philosophy, they alone really live; for they are not content to be good guardians of their own lifetime only. They annex every age to their own; all the years that have gone before them are an addition to their store. Unless we are most ungrateful, all those men, glorious fashioners of holy thoughts, were born for us; for us they have prepared a way of life. By other men's labours we are led to the sight of things most beautiful that have been wrested from darkness and brought into light; from no age are we shut out, we have access to all ages, and if it is our wish, by greatness of mind, to pass beyond the narrow limits of human weakness, there is a great stretch of time through which we may roam. We may argue with Socrates, we may doubt with Carneades, find peace with Epicurus, overcome human nature with the Stoics, exceed it with the Cynics. Since Nature allows us to enter into fellowship with every age, why should we not turn from this paltry and fleeting span of time and surrender ourselves with all our soul to the past, which is boundless, which is eternal, which we share with our betters?

—Lucius Annaeus Seneca.
On the Shortness of Life.

Philosophy is of two kinds: that which relates to conduct, and that which relates to knowledge. The first teaches us to value all things at their real worth, to be contented with little, modest in prosperity, patient in trouble, equal-minded at all times. It teaches us our duty to our neighbour and ourselves.

There may be wisdom without knowledge, and there may be knowledge without wisdom. A man without knowledge, if he walk humbly with his God, and live in charity with his neighbours, may be wise unto salvation. A man without wisdom may not find his knowledge avail him quite so well. But it is he who possesses both that is the true philosopher. The more he knows, the more he is desirous of knowing; and yet the farther he advances in knowledge the better he understands how little he can attain, and the more deeply he feels that God alone can satisfy the infinite desires of an immortal soul. To understand this is the height and perfection of philosophy.

—ROBERT SOUTHEY.
The Doctor, &c: In Two Volumes.

Philosopher, lover of wisdom, that is to say, of truth. All philosophers have had this dual character; there is not one in antiquity who has not given mankind examples of virtue and lessons in moral truths. They have all contrived to be deceived about natural philosophy; but natural philosophy is so little necessary for the conduct of life, that the philosophers had no need of it. It has taken centuries to learn a part of nature's laws. One day was sufficient for a wise man to learn the duties of man.

—VOLTAIRE.
Voltaire's Philosophical Dictionary.

O Philosophy, thou guide of life! thou discoverer of virtue and expeller of vices! what had not only I myself, but the whole life of man, been without you? To you it is that we owe the origin of cities; you it was who called together the dispersed race of men into social life;

You have been the inventress of laws; you have been our instructress in morals and discipline; to you we fly for refuge; from you we implore assistance; and as I formerly submitted to you in a great degree, so now I surrender up myself entirely to you. For one day spent well, and agreeably to your precepts, is preferable to an eternity of error.

—Marcus Tullius Cicero.
"Book V. Whether Virtue Alone Be Sufficient for A Happy Life." *Cicero's Tusculan Disputations.*

Chapter 4
ON WISDOM

Wisdom alone is true ambition's aim,
Wisdom the source of virtue, and of fame,
Obtained with labour, for mankind employed,
And then, when most you share it, best enjoyed.

—WILLIAM WHITEHEAD.
"On Nobility."

Approach it and you will not see a beginning;
follow it and there will be no end.
When we grasp the Tao of the ancient ones,
we can use it to direct our life today.
To know the ancient origin of Tao:
this is the beginning of wisdom.

—LAO TZU.
The Tao Te Ching.

To finish the moment, to find the journey's end in every step of the road, to live the greatest number of good hours, is wisdom.

—RALPH WALDO EMERSON.
"Experience." *Essays, Second Series.*

Happy is the man that findeth wisdom, and the man that getteth understanding.
For the merchandise of it is better than the merchandise of silver, and the gain thereof than fine gold.
She is more precious than rubies: and all the things thou canst desire are not to be compared unto her.
Length of days is in her right hand; and in her left hand riches and honour.
Her ways are ways of pleasantness, and all her paths are peace.
She is a tree of life to them that lay hold upon her: and happy is every one that retaineth her.

—PROVERBS 3:13-18. *KJV.*

Let no one be slow to seek wisdom when he is young nor weary in the search of it when he has grown old. For no age is too early or too late for the health of the soul. And to say that the season for studying philosophy has not yet come, or that it is past and gone, is like saying that the season for happiness is not yet or that it is now no more. Therefore, both old and young alike ought to seek wisdom, the former in order that, as age comes over him, he may be young in good things because of the grace of what has been, and the latter in order that, while he is young, he may at the same time be old, because he has no fear of the things which are to come. So we must exercise ourselves in the things which bring happiness, since, if that be present, we have everything, and, if that be absent, all our actions are directed towards attaining it.

—Epicurus.
Letter to Menoeceus.

The only medicine for suffering, crime, and all the woes of mankind, is wisdom.

—Thomas Huxley.
Aphorisms and Reflections.

Wisdom is the daughter of experience.
Learning acquired in youth arrests the evil of old age; and if you understand that old age has wisdom for its food, you will so conduct yourself in youth that your old age will not lack for nourishment.

—The Literary Works of Leonardo Da Vinci.

It is better to hear the rebuke of the wise, than for a man to hear the song of fools.

—Ecclesiastes 7:5. *KJV.*

Humbleness, truthfulness, and harmlessness,
Patience and honour, reverence for the wise.
Purity, constancy, control of self,
Contempt of sense-delights, self-sacrifice,
Perception of the certitude of ill
In birth, death, age, disease, suffering, and sin;
Detachment, lightly holding unto home,
Children, and wife, and all that bindeth men;
An ever-tranquil heart in fortunes good
And fortunes evil, with a will set firm
To worship Me—Me only! ceasing not;
Loving all solitudes, and shunning noise
Of foolish crowds; endeavours resolute
To reach perception of the Utmost Soul,
And grace to understand what gain it were
So to attain,—this is true Wisdom, Prince!
And what is otherwise is ignorance!

—THE BHAGAVAD-GITA.

To study the lives, to meditate the sorrows, to commune
with the thoughts, of the great and holy men and women
of this rich world is a sacred discipline.

—JAMES MARTINEAU.
Hours of Thought on Sacred Things. Volume 1.

There may be wisdom without knowledge, and there may be knowledge without wisdom. A man without knowledge, if he walk humbly with his God, and live in charity with his neighbours, may be wise unto salvation. A man without wisdom may not find his knowledge avail him quite so well.

—ROBERT SOUTHEY.
The Doctor, &c: In Two Volumes.

...and, first, of wisdom; not in the latitude of its various operations, but as it has only a regard to good life, and the happiness of mankind.

Wisdom is right understanding, a faculty of discerning good from evil; what is to be chosen; and what rejected; a judgment grounded upon the value of things, and not the common opinion of them; an equality of force, and a strength of resolution. It sets a watch over our words and deeds, it takes us up with the contemplation of the works of nature, and makes us invincible by either good or evil fortune.

—LUCIUS ANNAEUS SENECA.
"Of a Happy Life." *Seneca's Morals by Way of Abstract.*

It has taken centuries to learn a part of nature's laws. One day was sufficient for a wise man to learn the duties of man.

—VOLTAIRE.
The Philosophical Dictionary.

Be wise today; 'tis madness to defer.

—EDWARD YOUNG.

Night-Thoughts on Life, Death, and Immortality.

O world, thou choosest not the better part!
It is not wisdom to be only wise,
And on the inward vision close the eyes,
But it is wisdom to believe the heart.
Columbus found a world, and had no chart,
Save one that faith deciphered in the skies;
To trust the soul's invincible surmise
Was all his science and his only art.
Our knowledge is a torch of smoky pine
That lights the pathway but one step ahead
Across a void of mystery and dread.
Bid, then, the tender light of faith to shine
By which alone the mortal heart is led
Unto the thinking of the thought divine.

—GEORGE SANTAYANA.
"O World."

Chapter 5

ON PRAYER, MEDITATION, REFLECTION

What various hindrances we meet
In coming to a mercy seat!
Yet who that knows the worth of prayer,
But wishes to be often there?
Prayer makes the darken'd cloud withdraw,
Prayer climbs the ladder Jacob saw,
Gives exercise to faith and love,
Brings every blessing from above.

—WILLIAM COWPER.
"Exhortation to Prayer."

You pray in your distress and in your need; would that you might pray also in the fullness of your joy and in your days of abundance.

—KAHLIL GIBRAN.
The Prophet.

Give thyself more diligently to reflection: know thyself: take counsel with the Godhead: without God put thine hand unto nothing!

—EPICTETUS.
The Golden Sayings of Epictetus.

Flocks of birds have flown high and away;
A solitary drift of cloud, too, has gone, wandering on.
And I sit alone with the Ching-ting peak, towering beyond.
We never grow tired of other, the mountain and I.

—LI BAI.
"The Ching-ting Mountain."

It is prayer, meditation, and converse with God that refreshes, restores, and renews the temper of our minds, at all times, under all trials, after all conflicts with the world, when our own carnal will and frailty has betrayed us to our fall and breaches have been made in our most stedfast resolutions. By this contact with the world unseen we receive continual accesses of strength.

—HENRY EDWARD MANNING.
Sermons. Volume the Second.

The camel at the close of day
Kneels down upon the sandy plain
To have his burden lifted off

And rest again.
My soul, thou too shouldst to thy knees
When daylight draweth to a close,
And let thy Master lift thy load,
And grant repose.

Else how canst thou tomorrow meet,
With all tomorrow's work to do,
If thou thy burden all the night
Dost carry through?
The camel kneels at break of day
To have his guide replace his load,
Then rises up anew to take
The desert road.
So thou shouldst kneel at morning dawn
That God may give thy daily care,
Assured that he no load too great
Will make thee bear.

—ANNA TEMPLE.
"The Kneeling Camel."

What we need, then, is an attitude of prayer, in which we can *constantly* abide, and out of which exterior occupations cannot draw us; a prayer which can be offered alike by princes, kings, prelates, magistrates, soldiers, children, artisans, labourers, women, and the sick. This prayer is not mental, but *of the heart.*

—MADAME GUYON.
A Short Method of Prayer and Spiritual Torrents.

The Divine wisdom has given us prayer, not as a means whereby to obtain the good things of earth, but as a means whereby we learn to do without them; not as a means whereby we escape evil, but as a means whereby we become strong to meet it.

—Frederick William Robertson.
Sermons Preached at Trinity Chapel, Brighton:
Second Series, Volume 2.

Blessed is the man that walketh not in the counsel of the ungodly, nor standeth in the way of sinners, nor sitteth in the seat of the scornful.

But his delight is in the law of the LORD; and in his law doth he meditate day and night.

—Psalms 1:1-2. *KJV.*

Accustom yourself gradually to carry prayer into all your daily occupations. Speak, move, work, in peace, as if you were in prayer, as indeed you ought to be.

—Francois de Salignac de La Mothe Fénelon.
Selections from Fénelon.

One single grateful thought raised to heaven is the most perfect prayer.

—Gotthold Ephraim Lessing.
Minna von Barnhelm.

That prayer or inner communion with the spirit thereof—be that spirit 'God' or 'law'—is a process wherein work is really done, and spiritual energy flows in and produces effects, psychological or material, within the phenomenal world.

—WILLIAM JAMES.
The Varieties of Religious Experience.

Let me to-day do something that shall take
A little sadness from the world's vast store,
And may I be so favoured as to make
Of joy's too scanty sum a little more.
Let me not hurt, by any selfish deed
Or thoughtless word, the heart of foe or friend;
Nor would I pass, unseeing, worthy need,
Or sin by silence when I should defend.
However meagre be my worldly wealth
Let me give something that shall aid my kind,
A word of courage, or a thought of health,
Dropped as I pass for troubled hearts to find.
Let me to-night look back across the span
'Twixt dawn and dark, and to my conscience say—
Because of some good act to beast or man—
"The world is better that I lived to-day."

—ELLA WHEELER WILCOX.
"Morning Prayer."

To study the lives, to meditate the sorrows, to commune with the thoughts, of the great and holy men and women of this rich world, is a sacred discipline, which deserves at least to rank as the forecourt of the temple of true worship, and may train the tastes, ere we pass the very gate, of heaven. We forfeit the chief source of dignity and sweetness in life, next to the direct communion with God, if we do not seek converse with the greater minds that have left their vestiges on the world.

—James Martineau.
Hours of Thought on Sacred Things.

Be sure that you have made no small progress in the spiritual life, when you can control your imagination, so as to fix it on the duty and occupation actually existing, to the exclusion of the crowd of thoughts which are perpetually sweeping across the mind. No doubt, you cannot prevent those thoughts from arising, but you can prevent yourself from dwelling on them; you can put them aside, you can check the self-complacency, or irritation, or earthly longings which feed them, and by the practice of such control of your thoughts you will attain that spirit of inward silence which draws the soul into a close intercourse with God.

—Pere Jean Nicolas Grou.
The Hidden Life of the Soul.

Chapter 6

On the Still, Small Voice Within

Yet still there whispers the small voice within,
Heard through Gain's silence, and o'er Glory's din:
Whatever creed be taught or land be trod,
Man's conscience is the oracle of God!

—George Gordon Byron (Lord Byron).
The Island, or Christian and His Comrades.

It is a secret, hushed voice, a gentle intercourse of heart to heart, a still, small voice, whispering to the inner ear. How should we hear it, if we fill our ears and our hearts with the din of this world, its empty tumult, its excitement, its fretting vanities, or cares, or passions, or anxieties, or show, or rivalries, and its whirl of emptinesses?

—Edward Bouverie Pusey.
Parochial Sermons, Volume 2.

Though heralded with nought of fear,
Or outward sign or show:
Though only to the inward ear
It whispers soft and low;
Though dropping, as the manna fell,
Unseen, yet from above,
Noiseless as dew-fall, heed it well,—
Thy Father's call of love.

—JOHN GREENLEAF WHITTIER.
"The Call of the Christian."

Open, Lord, my inward ear,
And bid my heart rejoice;
Bid my quiet spirit hear
Thy comfortable voice;
Never in the whirlwind found,
Or where earthquakes rock the place,
Still and silent is the sound,
The whisper of thy grace.
From the world of sin, and noise, .
And hurry I withdraw;
For the small and inward voice
I wait with humble awe;
Silent am I now and still,
Dare not in thy presence move;
To my waiting soul reveal
The secret of thy love.

—CHARLES WESLEY.
"Waiting for Christ the Prophet."
Hymns and Sacred Poems.

There is hardly ever a complete silence in our souls. God is whispering to us wellnigh incessantly. Whenever the sounds of the world die out in the soul, or sink low, then we hear these whisperings of God. This is so invariable that we come to believe He is always whispering to us, only that we do not always hear, because of the noise, hurry, and distraction which life causes as it rushes on.

—FREDERICK WILLIAM FABER.
Spiritual Conferences.

We can't choose happiness either for ourselves or for another; we can't tell where that will lie. We can only choose whether we will indulge ourselves in the present moment, or whether we will renounce that, for the sake of obeying the Divine voice within us,- for the sake of being true to all the motives that sanctify our lives.

—GEORGE ELIOT.
The Mill on the Floss.

What we call Conscience is the voice of Divine love in the deep of our being, desiring union with our will.

—JAMES PIERREPONT GREAVES.
The Unity of Truth. A Devotional Diary.

Does anyone complain, that the best affections are transient visitors with him, and the heavenly spirit a stranger to his heart? Oh, let him not go forth, on any strained wing of thought, in distant quest of them; but rather stay at home, and set his house in the true order of conscience; and of their own accord the divinest guests will enter.

—James Martineau.
Endeavors After the Christian Life.

Thou shalt not heed the voice of man when it agrees not with the voice of God in thine own soul.

—Ralph Waldo Emerson.

Some call it the voice of the soul; some call it the voice of God; some call it the sixth sense. It is our inner spiritual sense.

In the degree that we come into the recognition of our own true selves, into the realization of the oneness of our life with the Infinite Life, and in the degree that we open ourselves to this divine inflow, does this voice of intuition, this voice of the soul, this voice of God, speak clearly; and in the degree that we recognize, listen to, and obey it, does it speak ever more clearly, until by-and-by there comes the time when it is unerring, absolutely unerring, in its guidance.

—Ralph Waldo Trine.
In Tune with the Infinite.

Be what it may, let the first whisper of the internal monitor be listened to as an oracle, as the still small voice which Elijah heard when he wrapped his face in his mantle, recognizing it to be the voice of God.

—ROBERT HALL.
The Works of the Rev. Robert Hall, Volume 2.

Alas, that we should be so unwilling to listen to the still and holy yearnings of the heart! A god whispers quite softly in our breast, softly yet audibly; telling us what we ought to seek and what to shun.

—JOHANN WOLFGANG VON GOETHE.
Torquato Tasso.

Conscience is the voice of the soul, the passions are the voice of the body. Is it astonishing that often these two languages contradict each other, and then to which must we listen? Too often reason deceives us; we have only too much acquired the right of refusing to listen to it; but conscience never deceives us; it is the true guide of man; it is to man what instinct is to the body, which follows it, obeys nature, and never is afraid of going astray.

—JEAN-JACQUES ROUSSEAU.
Emile.

Conscience is nothing else but the echo of God's voice within the soul.

—E. B. Hall.
Thoughts.

What Conscience dictates to be done,
Or warns me not to do;
This teach me more than Hell to shun,
That more than Heav'n pursue.

—Alexander Pope.
"Universal Prayer.

Part Two

ON THE NATURE
OF THINGS

Chapter 7

ON NATURE, THE WORLD, THE UNIVERSE

My heart leaps up when I behold
A rainbow in the sky;
So was it when my life began;
So is it now I am a man;
So be it when I shall grow old,
Or let me die!
The Child is father of the Man;
I could wish my days to be
Bound each to each by natural piety.

—WILLIAM WORDSWORTH.
"The Rainbow."

I cannot open my eyes without admiring the art that shines throughout all nature; the least cast suffices to make me perceive the Hand that makes everything.

Nay, what is called the art of men is but a faint imitation of the great art called the laws of Nature, and which the impious did not blush to call blind chance. Is it therefore a wonder that poets animated the whole universe, bestowed wings upon the winds, and arrows on the sun, and described great rivers impetuously running to precipitate themselves into the sea, and trees shooting up to heaven to repel the rays of the sun by their thick shades? These images and figures have also been received in the language of the vulgar, so natural it is for men to be sensible of the wonderful art that fills all nature. Poetry did only ascribe to inanimate creatures the art and design of the Creator, who does everything in them. From the figurative language of the poets those notions passed into the theology of the heathens, whose divines were the poets. They supposed an art, a power, or a wisdom, which they called *numen*, in creatures the most destitute of understanding. With them great rivers were gods; and springs, naiads. Woods and mountains had their particular deities; flowers had their Flora; and fruits, Pomona. After all, the more a man contemplates Nature, the more he discovers in it an inexhaustible stock of wisdom, which is, as it were, the soul of the universe.

—Francois de Salignac de La Mothe- Fénelon.
A Demonstration of the Existence and Attributes of God.

Give fools their gold, and knaves their power;
Let fortune's bubbles rise and fall;
Who sows a field, or trains a flower,
Or plants a tree, is more than all.

—John Greenleaf Whittier.
"A Song of Harvest."

A traveler met an old man planting a tree. "How foolish!" the traveler scoffed. "Surely you don't expect to live long enough to eat the fruit of that tree."

"Just as I found fruit trees when I came into the world," the old man replied, "so I am now planting trees for my children and grandchildren to enjoy."

—JEWISH FOLK TALE

I think that I shall never see
A poem lovely as a tree.
A tree whose hungry mouth is prest
Against the earth's sweet flowing breast;
A tree that looks at God all day,
And lifts her leafy arms to pray;
A tree that may in summer wear
A nest of robins in her hair;
Upon whose bosom snow has lain;
Who intimately lives with rain.
Poems are made by fools like me,
But only God can make a tree.

—JOYCE KILMER.
"Trees."

The world of dew
Is the world of dew,
And yet, and yet –

—KOBAYASHI ISSA.

The world globes itself in a drop of dew. The microscope cannot find the animalcule which is less perfect for being little. Eyes, ears, taste, smell, motion, resistance, appetite, and organs of reproduction that take hold on eternity,—all find room to consist in the small creature. So do we put our life into every act. The true doctrine of omnipresence is that God reappears with all his parts in every moss and cobweb. The value of the universe contrives to throw itself into every point.

—RALPH WALDO EMERSON.
"Compensation." *Essays, First Series.*

You never enjoy the world aright, till the Sea itself floweth in your veins, till you are clothed with the heavens, and crowned with the stars: and perceive yourself to be the sole heir of the whole world, and more than so, because men are in it who are every one sole heirs as well as you. Till you can sing and rejoice and delight in God, as misers do in gold, and Kings in sceptres, you never enjoy the world.

Till your spirit filleth the whole world, and the stars are your jewels; till you are as familiar with the ways of God in all Ages as with your walk and table: till you are intimately acquainted with that shady nothing out of which the world was made: till you love men so as to desire their happiness, with a thirst equal to the zeal of your own: till you delight in God for being good to all: you never enjoy the world.

—THOMAS TRAHERNE.
Centuries of Meditations.

Before the universe was born
there was something in the chaos of the heavens.
It stands alone and empty,
solitary and unchanging.
It is ever present and secure.
It may be regarded as the Mother of the universe.
Because I do not know its name,
I call it the Tao.
If forced to give it a name,
I would call it 'Great'.
Because it is Great means it is everywhere.
Being everywhere means it is eternal.
Being eternal means everything returns to it.

—LAO TZU.
The Tao Te Ching.

Enlightenment is like the moon reflected on the water.
The moon does not get wet, nor is the water broken.
Although its light is wide and great,
The moon is reflected even in a puddle an inch wide.
The whole moon and the entire sky
Are reflected in one dewdrop on the grass,
Or even in one drop of water.
Enlightenment does not divide you,
Just as the moon does not break the water.
You cannot hinder enlightenment,
Just as a drop of water does not hinder the moon in the sky

—DOGEN ZENJI.
"Genjo Koan."

It is not raining rain for me,
It's raining daffodils;
In every dimpled drop I see
Wild flowers on the hills.
The clouds of gray engulf the day
And overwhelm the town;
It is not raining rain to me,
It's raining roses down.
It is not raining rain to me,
But fields of clover bloom,
Where any buccaneering bee
Can find a bed and room.
A health unto the happy,
A fig for him who frets!
It is not raining rain to me,
It's raining violets.

—Robert Loveman.
"April Rain."

It is, indeed, but a feeble expression of the truth to say that the infinities revealed to us by Science, –the infinitely great in the one direction, and the infinitely small in the other, –go far beyond anything which had occurred to the unaided imagination of Man, and are not only a never-failing source of pleasure and interest, but seem to lift us out of the petty troubles and sorrows of life.

—Sir John Lubbock.
"The Beauties of Nature." *The Pleasures of Life: Part II.*

The study of cause and effect, while it lessens the painfulness of life, adds to life's picturesqueness. The man to whom evolution is but a name looks at the sea as a grandiose, monotonous spectacle, which he can witness in August for three shillings third-class return. The man who is imbued with the idea of development, of continuous cause and effect, perceives in the sea an element which in the day-before-yesterday of geology was vapour, which yesterday was boiling, and which to-morrow will inevitably be ice. He perceives that a liquid is merely something on its way to be solid, and he is penetrated by a sense of the tremendous, changeful picturesqueness of life. Nothing will afford a more durable satisfaction than the constantly cultivated appreciation of this. It is the end of all science.

—ARNOLD BENNETT.
How to Live on Twenty-four Hours a Day.

Do you see this grain of sand
Lying loosely in my hand?
Do you know to me it brought
Just a simple loving thought?
When one gazes night by night
On the glorious stars of light,
Oh how little seems the span
Measured round the life of man.
Oh! how fleeting are his years
With their smiles and their tears;
Can it be that God does care
For such atoms as we are?
Then outspake this grain of sand

'I was fashioned by His hand
In the star lit realms of space
I was made to have a place.

—FRANCES ELLEN WATKINS HARPER.
"A Grain of Sand."

To see a World in a Grain of Sand
And a Heaven in a Wild Flower,
Hold Infinity in the palm of your hand
And Eternity in an hour.

—WILLIAM BLAKE.
"Auguries of Innocence."

How could the richer animistic aspects of Nature, the peculiarities and oddities that make phenomena picturesquely striking or expressive, fail to have been first singled out and followed by philosophy as the more promising avenue to the knowledge of Nature's life? Well, it is still in these richer animistic and dramatic aspects that religion delights to dwell. It is the terror and beauty of phenomena, the 'promise' of the dawn and of the rainbow, the 'voice' of the thunder, the 'gentleness' of the summer rain, the 'sublimity' of the stars, and not the physical laws which these things follow, by which the religious mind still continues to be most impressed; and just as of yore, the devout man tells you that in the solitude of his room or of the fields he still feels the divine presence, that inflowings of help come in reply to his prayers, and that sacrifices to this unseen reality fill him with security and peace.

—WILLIAM JAMES.
The Varieties of Religious Experience.

You are a child of the universe,
no less than the trees and the stars;
you have a right to be here.
And whether or not it is clear to you,
no doubt the universe is unfolding as it should.

—MAX EHRMANN.
"Desiderata."

A haze on the far horizon,
The infinite, tender sky,
The ripe, rich tint of the cornfields,
And the wild geese sailing high,—
And all over the upland and lowland
The charm of the goldenrod,—
Some of us call it Autumn,
And others call it God.

—WILLIAM HERBERT CARRUTH.
"Each In His Own Tongue."

Chapter 8

ON THE ETERNAL, THE ABSOLUTE, THE UNKNOWABLE

All things are created by the Om;
The love-form is His body.
He is without form, without quality, without decay:
Seek thou union with Him!
But that formless God takes a thousand forms in the eyes of His creatures:
He is pure and indestructible,
His form is infinite and fathomless,
He dances in rapture, and waves of form arise from His dance.
The body and the mind cannot contain themselves, when they are touched by His great joy.
He is immersed in all consciousness, all joys, and all sorrows;
He has no beginning and no end;
He holds all within His bliss.

—SONGS OF KABIR.

The Absolute is never born, never dead. It comes out of nothing and goes into nothing.—It is unborn, eternal, immutable, ever unique, never destroyed with the destruction of the body.

—"Kathopanishad."
The Spirit of the Upanishads
(or the Aphorisms of the Wise).

Before the universe was born
there was something in the chaos of the heavens.
It stands alone and empty,
solitary and unchanging.
It is ever present and secure.
It may be regarded as the Mother of the universe.
Because I do not know its name,
I call it the Tao.
If forced to give it a name,
I would call it 'Great'.
Because it is Great means it is everywhere.
Being everywhere means it is eternal.
Being eternal means everything returns to it.

—*Tao Te Ching by Lao-Tzu.*

For in fact what is man in nature? A Nothing in comparison with the Infinite, an All in comparison with the Nothing, a mean between nothing and everything. Since he is infinitely removed from comprehending the extremes, the end of things and their beginning are hopelessly hidden from him in an impenetrable secret, he is equally incapable of seeing the Nothing from which he was made, and the Infinite in which he is swallowed up.

What will he do then, but perceive the appearance of the middle of things, in an eternal despair of knowing either their beginning or their end. All things proceed from the Nothing, and are borne towards the Infinite. Who will follow these marvelous processes? The Author of these wonders understands them. None other can do so.

—BLAISE PASCAL.
Pensées (Thoughts).

As light belongs to the sun, coldness to water, and heat to fire, so do existence, consciousness, bliss, eternity, immutable purity, belong by nature, to That.

—ATMABODHA.
The Spirit of the Upanishads
(or the Aphorisms of the Wise).

That which cannot be seen, nor seized, which has no family and no caste, no eyes nor ears, no hands nor feet, the eternal, the omnipresent (all-pervading), infinitesimal, that which is imperishable, that it is which the wise regard as the source of all beings.

As the spider sends forth and draws in its thread, as plants grow on the earth, as from every man hairs spring forth on the head and the body, thus does everything arise here from the Indestructible.

—"Mundaka Upanishad I.1.6-7."

…let that vain struggle to read the mystery of the infinite cease to harass us. It is a mystery which, through all ages we shall only read here a line of, there a line of.

—Thomas Carlyle.
"Characteristics."

Know, too, from Me
Shineth the gathered glory of the suns
Which lighten all the world: from Me the moons
Draw silvery beams, and fire fierce loveliness.
I penetrate the clay, and lend all shapes
Their living force; I glide into the plant—
Root, leaf, and bloom—to make the woodlands green
With springing sap.

—The Bhagavad-Gita.

The whole visible world is only an imperceptible atom in the ample bosom of nature. No idea approaches it. We may enlarge our conceptions beyond all imaginable space; we only produce atoms in comparison with the reality of things. It is an infinite sphere, the centre of which is everywhere, the circumference nowhere. In short it is the greatest sensible mark of the almighty power of God, that imagination loses itself in that thought.

—BLAISE PASCAL.
Pensées (Thoughts).

The tao that can be described
is not the eternal Tao.
The name that can be spoken
is not the eternal Name.
The nameless is the boundary of Heaven and Earth.
The named is the mother of creation.
Freed from desire, you can see the hidden mystery.
By having desire, you can only see what is visibly real.
Yet mystery and reality
emerge from the same source.

—*TAO TE CHING BY LAO-TZU.*

Chapter 9

ON HIGHER LAWS, DIVINE ORDER, THE NATURE OF THINGS, FATE

'Tis Providence alone secures
In every change both mine and yours:
Safety consists not in escape
From dangers of a frightful shape;
An earthquake may be bid to spare
The man that's strangled by a hair.
Fate steals along with silent tread,
Found oft'nest in what least we dread,
Frowns in the storm with angry brow,
But in the sunshine strikes the blow.

—WILLIAM COWPER.
"The Fable."

A little consideration of what takes place around us every day would show us that a higher law than that of our will regulates events; that our painful labors are unnecessary and fruitless; that only in our easy, simple, spontaneous action are we strong, and by contenting ourselves with obedience we become divine.

—RALPH WALDO EMERSON.
"Spiritual Laws." *Essays, First Series.*

Were one asked to characterize the life of religion in the broadest and most general terms possible, one might say that it consists of the belief that there is an unseen order, and that our supreme good lies in harmoniously adjusting ourselves thereto. This belief and this adjustment are the religious attitude in the soul.

—WILLIAM JAMES.
The Varieties of Religious Experience.

On two days it steads not to run from thy grave,
The appointed, and the unappointed day;
On the first, neither balm nor physician can save,
Nor thee, on the second, the Universe slay.

—RALPH WALDO EMERSON.
"Ali Ben Abu Taleb." *Poems/Translations.*

What fates impose, that men must needs abide;
It boots not to resist both wind and tide.

—WILLIAM SHAKESPEARE.
Henry VI, Part 3.

Let us build to the Beautiful Necessity, which makes man brave in believing that he cannot shun a danger that is appointed, nor incur one that is not; to the Necessity which rudely or softly educates him to the perception that there are no contingencies; that Law rules throughout existence, a Law which is not intelligent but intelligence,—not personal nor impersonal,—it disdains words and passes understanding; it dissolves persons; it vivifies nature; yet solicits the pure in heart to draw on all its omnipotence.

—RALPH WALDO EMERSON.
"Fate." *The Conduct of Life.*

Concerning the Gods, there are those who deny the very existence of the Godhead; others say that it exists, but neither bestirs nor concerns itself nor has forethought for anything. A third party attribute to it existence and forethought, but only for great and heavenly matters, not for anything that is on earth. A fourth party admit things on earth as well as in heaven, but only in general, and not with respect to each individual. A fifth, of whom were Ulysses and Socrates, are those that cry: - I move not without Thy knowledge!

—*THE GOLDEN SAYINGS OF EPICTETUS.*

The intuition of the moral sentiment is an insight of the perfection of the laws of the soul. These laws execute themselves. They are out of time, out of space, and not subject to circumstance. Thus; in the soul of man there is a justice whose retributions are instant and entire. He who does a good deed, is instantly ennobled. He who does a mean deed, is by the action itself contracted. He who puts off impurity, thereby puts on purity.

—RALPH WALDO EMERSON.
The Divinity School Address.

Life is a series of surprises. We do not guess to-day the mood, the pleasure, the power of to-morrow, when we are building up our being. Of lower states, of acts of routine and sense, we can tell somewhat; but the masterpieces of God, the total growths and universal movements of the soul, he hideth; they are incalculable. I can know that truth is divine and helpful; but how it shall help me I can have no guess, for so to be is the sole inlet of so to know.

—RALPH WALDO EMERSON.
"Circles." *Essays, First Series.*

With constant motion as the moments glide.
Behold in running life the rolling tide!
For none can stem by art, or stop by pow'r,
The flowing ocean, or the fleeting hour:
But wave by wave pursued arrives on shore,
And each impell'd behind impels before:

So time on time revolving we descry;
So minutes follow, and so minutes fly.

—OVID.
Metamorphoses, XV. 179.

Presumptuous man! the reason wouldst thou find,
Why formed so weak, so little, and so blind?
First, if thou canst, the harder reason guess,
Why formed no weaker, blinder, and no less;
Ask of thy mother earth, why oaks are made
Taller or stronger than the weeds they shade?
Or ask of yonder argent fields above,
Why Jove's satellites are less than Jove?
Of systems possible, if 'tis confest
That wisdom infinite must form the best

—ALEXANDER POPE.
An Essay on Man.

The life, the fortune, and the happiness of every one of us, and, more or less, of those who are connected with us, do depend upon our knowing something of the rules of a game infinitely more difficult and complicated than chess. It is a game which has been played for untold ages, every man and woman of us being one of the two players in a game of his or her own. The chessboard is the world, the pieces are the phenomena of the universe, the rules of the game are what we call the laws of Nature. The player on the other side is hidden from us. We know that his play is always fair, just and patient. But also we know, to our cost, that he never overlooks a mistake, or makes the smallest allowance for ignorance. To the man who plays well, the highest stakes are paid, with that sort of overflowing generosity with which the strong shows delight in strength. And one who plays ill is checkmated–without haste, but without remorse.

—THOMAS HUXLEY.
Aphorisms and Reflections

Hast not thy share? On winged feet,
Lo! it rushes thee to meet;
And all that Nature made thy own,
Floating in air or pent in stone,
Will rive the hills and swim the sea
And, like thy shadow, follow thee.

—RALPH WALDO EMERSON.
"Compensation." *Essays, First Series.*

If Nature thundered in his opening ears,
And stunned him with the music of the spheres,
How would he wish that Heaven had left him still
The whispering zephyr, and the purling rill?
Who finds not Providence all good and wise,
Alike in what it gives, and what it denies?

—ALEXANDER POPE.
An Essay on Man.

Man is a stream whose source is hidden. Our being is descending into us from we know not whence. The most exact calculator has no prescience that somewhat incalculable may not balk the very next moment. I am constrained every moment to acknowledge a higher origin for events than the will I call mine.

—RALPH WALDO EMERSON.
"The Over-Soul." *Essays, First Series.*

On the whole, as this wondrous planet, Earth, is journeying with its fellows through infinite Space, so are the wondrous destinies embarked on it journeying through infinite Time, under a higher guidance than ours.

—THOMAS CARLYLE.
"Signs of the Times."

Joy and anger, sorrow and happiness, caution and remorse, come upon us by turns, with ever-changing mood. They come like music from hollowness, like mushrooms from damp. Daily and nightly they alternate within us, but we cannot tell whence they spring. Can we then hope in a moment to lay our finger upon their very Cause?

But for these emotions *I* should not be. But for *me*, they would have no scope. So far we can go; but we do not know what it is that brings them into play. 'Twould seem to be a *soul;* but the clue to its existence is wanting. That such a Power operates, is credible enough, though we cannot see its form. It has functions without form.

—CHUANG TZŬ.
Chuang Tzŭ, Mystic, Moralist, and Social Reformer.

There is a divine sequence running throughout the universe. Within and above and below the human will incessantly works the Divine will. To come into harmony with it and thereby with all the higher laws and forces, to come then into league and to work in conjunction with them, in order that they can work in league and in conjunction with us, is to come into the chain of this wonderful sequence. This is the secret of all success. This is to come into the possession of unknown riches, into the realization of undreamed-of powers.

—RALPH WALDO TRINE.
In Tune with the Infinite.

Chapter 10

ON IMPERMANENCE, MORTALITY, THE MARCH OF TIME

It is time to be old,
To take in sail: -
The gods of bounds,
Who sets to seas a shore,
Came to me in his fatal rounds,
And said: 'No more!

As the bird trims her to the gale,
I trim myself to the storm of time,
I man the rudder, reef the sail,
Obey the voice at eve obeyed at prime:
'Lowly faithful, banish fear,
Right onward drive unharmed;
The port, well worth the cruise, is near,
And every wave is charmed.'

—RALPH WALDO EMERSON.
"Terminus."

Often think of the rapidity with which things pass by and disappear, both the things which are and the things which are produced. For substance is like a river in a continual flow, and the activities of things are in constant change, and the causes work in infinite varieties; and there is hardly anything which stands still. And consider this which is near to thee, this boundless abyss of the past and of the future in which all things disappear. How then is he not a fool who is puffed up with such things or plagued about them and makes himself miserable? For they vex him only for a time, and a short time.

—MARCUS AURELIUS.
The Meditations of Marcus Aurelius.

Life is real! Life is earnest!
And the grave is not its goal;
Dust thou art, to dust returnest,
Was not spoken of the soul.

—HENRY WADSWORTH LONGFELLOW.
"A Psalm of Life."

Pass then through this little space of time conformably to nature, and end thy journey in content, just as an olive falls off when it is ripe, blessing nature who produced it, and thanking the tree on which it grew.

—MARCUS AURELIUS.
The Meditations of Marcus Aurelius.

I follow and obey Nature, the surest guide, as if she were a god, and it is utterly improbable that she has well arranged the other parts of life, and yet, like an unskilled poet, slighted the last act of the drama. There must, however, of necessity, be some end, and, as in the case of berries on the trees and the fruits of the earth, there must be that which in its season of full ripeness is, so to speak, ready to wither and fall,—which a wise man ought to bear patiently.

—CICERO.
De Senectute (On Old Age).

The snow is fled: the trees their leaves put on,
The fields their green:
Earth owns the change, and rivers lessening run
Their banks between.
Naked the Nymphs and Graces in the meads
The dance essay:
"No 'scaping death" proclaims the year, that speeds
This sweet spring day.
Frosts yield to zephyrs; Summer drives out Spring,
To vanish, when
Rich Autumn sheds his fruits; round wheels the ring,—
Winter again!

—HORACE.
"Odes 4.7." *The Odes and Carmen Saeculare of Horace.*

The bell doth toll for him, that thinks it doth; and though it intermit again, yet from that minute, that that occasion wrought upon him, he is united to God. Who casts not up his eye to the sun when it rises? But who takes off his eye from a comet, when that breaks out? Who bends not his ear to any bell, which upon any occasion rings? But who can remove it from that bell, which is passing a piece of himself out of this world?

No man is an island, entire of itself; every man is a piece of the continent, a part of the main; if a clod be washed away by the sea, Europe is the less, as well as if a promontory were, as well as if a manor of thy friend's or of thine own were; any man's death diminishes me, because I am involved in mankind, and therefore never send to know for whom the bell tolls; it tolls for thee.

—JOHN DONNE.
"Meditation XVII. Devotions Upon Emergent Occasions."
The Works of John Donne. Volume 3.

For as with the close of the day, so with that of life; there may be clouds, and yet if the horizon is clear, the evening may be beautiful.

—SIR JOHN LUBBOCK.
"The Destiny of Man." *The Pleasures of Life.*

As the long train
Of ages glide away, the sons of men,

The youth in life's green spring, and he who goes
In the full strength of years, matron and maid,
The speechless babe, and the gray-headed man—
Shall one by one be gathered to thy side,
By those, who in their turn shall follow them.
So live, that when thy summons comes to join
The innumerable caravan, which moves
To that mysterious realm, where each shall take
His chamber in the silent halls of death,
Thou go not, like the quarry-slave at night,
Scourged to his dungeon, but, sustained and soothed
By an unfaltering trust, approach thy grave,
Like one who wraps the drapery of his couch
About him, and lies down to pleasant dreams.

—WILLIAM CULLEN BRYANT.
"Thanatopsis."

But since our life so fast away doth slide,
As doth a hungry eagle through the wind,
Or as a ship transported with the tide,
Which in their passage leave no print behind:
Of which swift little time so much we spend,
While some few things we through the sense do straine,
That our short race of life is at an end,
Ere we the principles of skill attaine.

—SIR JOHN DAVIES.
"The Immortality of the Soul."

Though heaven and earth are eternal, we are not born again. Human life is short at the longest; nothing flies more swiftly than time. Therefore, those who have been fortunate enough to see the light should make the most of life; they should consider how miserable it is to whistle their days away.

—HUNG YING-MING.
Musings of a Chinese Vegetarian.

When o'er the heaven Phoebus from his rose-red car begins to shed his light abroad, his flames oppress the paling stars and blunt their whitened rays. When the grove grows bright in spring with roses 'neath the west wind's warming breath, let but the cloudy gale once wildly blow, and their beauty is gone, the thorns alone remain. Often the sea is calmly glistening bright with all untroubled waves, but as often does the north wind stir them up, making the troubling tempest boil. If then the earth's own covering so seldom constant stays, if its changes are so great, shalt thou trust the brittle fortunes of mankind, have faith in fleeting good? For this is sure, and this is fixed by everlasting law, that naught which is brought to birth shall constant here abide.

—BOETHIUS.
The Consolation of Philosophy.

I mourn no more my vanished years
Beneath a tender rain,
An April rain of smiles and tears,
My heart is young again.

—JOHN GREENLEAF WHITTIER.
"My Psalm."

Our life is a warfare, and a mere pilgrimage. Fame after life is no better than oblivion. What is it then that will adhere and follow? Only one thing, philosophy. And philosophy doth consist in this, for a man to preserve that spirit which is within him, from all manner of contumelies and injuries, and above all pains or pleasures; never to do anything either rashly, or feignedly, or hypocritically: wholly to depend from himself and his own proper actions: all things that happen unto him to embrace contentedly, as coming from Him from whom he himself also came; and above all things, with all meekness and a calm cheerfulness, to expect death, as being nothing else but the resolution of those elements, of which every creature is composed. And if the elements themselves suffer nothing by this their perpetual conversion of one into another, that dissolution, and alteration, which is so common unto all, why should it be feared by any? Is not this according to nature?

—MARCUS AURELIUS.
The Meditations of Marcus Aurelius.

The work is finish'd, which nor dreads the rage
Of tempests, fire, or war, or wasting age;
Come, soon or late, death's undetermin'd day,
This mortal being only can decay;
My nobler part, my fame, shall reach the skies,
And to late times with blooming honours rise:
Whate'er th' unbounded Roman power obeys,
All climes and nations shall record my praise:
If 'tis allow'd to poets to divine,
One half of round eternity is mine.

—OVID.
Metamorphoses, XV.

Chapter 11

ON UNITY, ONENESS, YIN/YANG

Father of all! In every age,
In ev'ry clime ador'd,
By saint, by savage, and by sage,
Jehovah, Jove, or Lord!

—ALEXANDER POPE.
"Universal Prayer."

There is a golden thread that runs through every religion in the world. There is a golden thread that runs through the lives and the teachings of all the prophets, seers, sages, and saviours in the world's history, through the lives of all men and women of truly great and lasting power. All that they have ever done or attained to has been done in full accordance with law. What one has done, all may do.

This same golden thread must enter into the lives of all who today, in this busy work-a-day world of ours, would exchange impotence for power, weakness and suffering for abounding health and strength, pain and unrest for perfect peace, poverty of whatever nature for fullness and plenty.

—RALPH WALDO TRINE. *In Tune with the Infinite.*

We live in succession, in division, in parts, in particles. Meantime within man is the soul of the whole; the wise silence; the universal beauty, to which every part and particle is equally related; the eternal ONE. And this deep power in which we exist and whose beatitude is all accessible to us, is not only self- sufficing and perfect in every hour, but the act of seeing and the thing seen, the seer and the spectacle, the subject and the object, are one.

—RALPH WALDO EMERSON.
"The Over-Soul." *Essays, First Series.*

Thus revering the soul, and learning, as the ancient said, that "its beauty is immense, man will come to see that the world is the perennial miracle which the soul worketh, and be less astonished at particular wonders; he will learn that there is no profane history; that all history is sacred; that the universe is represented in an atom, in a moment of time. He will weave no longer a spotted life of shreds and patches, but he will live with a divine unity. He will cease from what is base and frivolous in his life and be content with all places and with any service he can render.

—RALPH WALDO EMERSON.
"The Over-Soul." *Essays, First Series.*

These facts have always suggested to man the sublime creed, that the world is not the product of manifold power, but of one will, of one mind; and that one mind is everywhere active, in each ray of the star, in each wavelet of the pool;

and whatever opposes that will, is everywhere balked and baffled, because things are made so, and not otherwise. Good is positive. Evil is merely privative, not absolute: it is like cold, which is the privation of heat. All evil is so much death or nonentity. Benevolence is absolute and real. So much benevolence as a man hath, so much life hath he. For all things proceed out of this same spirit, which is differently named love, justice, temperance, in its different applications, just as the ocean receives different names on the several shores which it washes. All things proceed out of the same spirit, and all things conspire with it.

—RALPH WALDO EMERSON. *The Divinity School Address.*

Like the bee, gathering honey from different flowers, the wise man accepts the essence of different scriptures and sees only the good in all religions.

—HINDUISM. *Srimad Bhagavatam 11.3*

The Tao gave birth to One.
The One gave birth to Two.
The Two gave birth to Three.
The Three gave birth to all of creation.
All things carry Yin
yet embrace Yang.
They blend their life breaths
in order to produce harmony.

—*TAO TE CHING* BY LAO-TZU.

The fountains mingle with the river
And the rivers with the ocean,
The winds of heaven mix for ever
With a sweet emotion;
Nothing in the world is single,
All things by a law divine
In one another's being mingle—
Why not I with thine?

—PERCY BYSSHE SHELLEY.
"Love's Philosophy."

Since everything then is cause and effect, dependent and supporting, mediate and immediate, and all is held together by a natural though imperceptible chain, which binds together things most distant and most different, I hold it equally impossible to know the parts without knowing the whole, and to know the whole without knowing the parts in detail.

—BLAISE PASCAL.
Pensées (Thoughts).

The great central fact of the universe is that Spirit of Infinite Life and Power that is behind all, that animates all, that manifests itself in and through all; that self-existent principle of life from which all has come, and not only from which all has come, but from which all is continually coming. If there is an individual life, there must of necessity be an infinite source of life from which it comes. If there is a quality or a force of love, there must of necessity be an infinite source of love whence it comes. If there is wisdom, there must be the all-wise source behind it from which it springs. The same is true in regard to peace, the same in regard to power, the same in regard to what we call material things.

—RALPH WALDO TRINE.
In Tune with the Infinite.

In the light of the silent stars that shine on the struggling sea,
In the weary cry of the wind and the whisper of flower and tree,
Under the breath of laughter, deep in the tide of tears,
I hear the Loom of the Weaver that weaves the Web of Years.

The leaves of the winter wither and sink in the forest mould
To colour the flowers of April with purple and white and gold:
Light and scent and music die and are born again
In the heart of a grey-haired woman who wakes in a world of pain.

The green uncrumpling fern and the rustling dewdrenched rose
Pass with our hearts to the Silence where the wings of music close,
Pass and pass to the Timeless that never a moment mars,
Pass and pass to the Darkness that made the suns and stars.

O, woven in one wide Loom thro' the throbbing weft of the whole,

One in spirit and flesh, one in body and soul,
Tho' the leaf were alone in its falling, the bird in its hour
to die,
The heart in its muffled anguish, the sea in its
mournful cry,

One with the flower of a day, one with the withered moon
One with the granite mountains that melt into the noon
One with the dream that triumphs beyond the light of
the spheres,
We come from the Loom of the Weaver that weaves the
Web of Years.

—ALFRED NOYES.
"The Loom of Years."

To regard the soul and body as one, or to ascribe to consciousness a physiological origin, is not detracting from its divinity, it is rather conferring divinity upon the body. One thing is inevitably linked with another – the higher forms with the lower forms, the butterfly with the grub, the flower with the root, the food we eat with the thought we think, the poem we write, or the picture we paint, with the processes of digestion and nutrition. How science has enlarged and ennobled and purified our conception of the universe; how it has cleaned out the evil spirits that have so long terrified mankind, and justified the verdict of the Creator: "and behold it was good"! With its indestructibility of matter, its conservation of energy, its inviolability of cause and effect, its unity of force and elements throughout sidereal space, it has prepared the way for a conception of man, his origin, his development, and in a measure his destiny, that at last makes him at home in the universe.

—JOHN BURROUGHS.
"The Divine Soil." *Leaf and Tendril.*

Chapter 12

On Rhythms, Ebb and Flow, Cycles

The day is cold, and dark, and dreary
It rains, and the wind is never weary;
The vine still clings to the mouldering wall,
But at every gust the dead leaves fall,
And the day is dark and dreary.
My life is cold, and dark, and dreary;
It rains, and the wind is never weary;
My thoughts still cling to the mouldering Past,
But the hopes of youth fall thick in the blast,
And the days are dark and dreary.
Be still, sad heart! and cease repining;
Behind the clouds is the sun still shining;
Thy fate is the common fate of all,
Into each life some rain must fall,
Some days must be dark and dreary.

—Henry Wadsworth Longfellow.
"The Rainy Day."

These alternations of happiness and depression are primarily manifestations of that law of periodicity, or law of rhythm, which guides the universe. Night and day alternate in the physical life of man as do happiness and depression in his emotional life. As the ebb and flow in the ocean, so are the ebb and flow in human feelings. There are tides in the human heart as in the affairs of men and as in the sea.

—ANNIE BESANT.
"Some Difficulties of the Inner Life."
Some Problems of Life.

As the rose-tree is composed of the sweetest flowers, and the sharpest thorns; as the heavens are sometimes fair, and sometimes overcast, alternately tempestuous and serene; so is the life of man intermingled with hopes and fears, with joys and sorrows, with pleasures and with pains.

—ROBERT BURTON.
The Anatomy of Melancholy…Being an Abridgment of Burton's Celebrated Work.

Joy and anger, sorrow and happiness, caution and remorse, come upon us by turns, with ever-changing mood. They come like music from hollowness, like mushrooms from damp. Daily and nightly they alternate within us, but we cannot tell whence they spring. Can we then hope in a moment to lay our finger upon their very Cause?

But for these emotions *I* should not be. But for *me*, they would have no scope. So far we can go; but we do not know what it is that brings them into play. 'Twould seem to be a *soul;* but the clue to its existence is wanting. That such a Power operates, is credible enough, though we cannot see its form. It has functions without form.

—Chuang Tzŭ.
Chuang Tzŭ, Mystic, Moralist, and Social Reformer.

It is right it should be so;
Man was made for joy and woe;
And when this we rightly know,
Thro' the world we safely go.
Joy and woe are woven fine,
A clothing for the soul divine.
Under every grief and pine
Runs a joy with silken twine.

—William Blake.
"Auguries of Innocence."

Good and ill seems as necessary to human life as light and shade are to a picture. We grow weary of uniform success, and pleasure soon surfeits. Pain makes ease delightful; hunger relishes the homeliest food, fatigue turns the hardest bed to down; and the difficulty and uncertainty of pursuits in all cases enhanced the value of possession.

—William Hazlitt.
"CCLXXXVII." *Characteristics: in the manner of*
Rochefoucault's Maxims.

When auburn Autumn mounts the stage,
And Summer fails her charms to yield,
Bleak nature turns another page,
To light the glories of the field.
At once the vale declines to bloom,
The forest smiles no longer gay;
Gardens are left without perfume,
The rose and lilly pine away.
The orchard bows her fruitless head,
As one divested of her store;
Or like a queen whose train has fled,
And left her sad to smile no more.
That bird which breath'd her vernal song,
And hopp'd along the flow'ry spray,
Now silent holds her warbling tongue,
Which dulcifies the feast of May.
But let each bitter have its sweet,
No change of nature is in vain;
'Tis just alternate cold and heat,
For time is pleasure mix'd with pain.

—GEORGE MOSES HORTON.
"Departing Summer."

The snow is fled: the trees their leaves put on,
The fields their green:
Earth owns the change, and rivers lessening run
Their banks between.
Naked the Nymphs and Graces in the meads
The dance essay:
"No 'scaping death" proclaims the year, that speeds

This sweet spring day.
Frosts yield to zephyrs; Summer drives out Spring,
To vanish, when
Rich Autumn sheds his fruits; round wheels the ring, -
Winter again!

—HORACE.
"Odes 4.7." *The Odes and Carmen Saeculare of Horace.*

But, as we use our brightest colours in a picture, so in the mind we ought to look at the cheerful and bright side of things, and hide and keep down the gloomy, for we cannot altogether obliterate or get rid of it. For, as the strings of the bow and lyre are alternately tightened and relaxed, so is it with the order of the world; in human affairs there is nothing pure and without alloy. But as in music there are high and low notes, and in grammar vowels and mutes, but neither the musician nor grammarian decline to use either kinds, but know how to blend and employ them both for their purpose, so in human affairs which are balanced one against another,-for, as Euripides says,

"There is no good without ill in the world, but everything is mixed in due proportion,"-we ought not to be disheartened or despondent; but as musicians drown their worst music with the best, so should we take good and bad together, and make our chequered life one of convenience and harmony.

—PLUTARCH.
"On Contentedness of Mind."
Plutarch's Morals: Ethical Essays.

Still, where rosy Pleasure leads,
See a kindred Grief pursue;
Behind the steps that Misery treads,
Approaching Comfort view:
The hues of bliss more brightly glow,
Chastis'd by sabler tints of woe;
And blended form, with artful strife,
The strength and harmony of life.
See the wretch, that long has tost
On the thorny bed of pain,
At length repair his vigour lost,
And breathe, and walk again:
The meanest flow'ret of the vale,
The simplest note that swells the gale,
The common sun, the air, the skies,
To him are opening Paradise.

—THOMAS GRAY.
"Ode on the Pleasure Arising from Vicissitude."

Being and non-being produce each other.
Difficult and easy complement each other.
Long and short define each other.
High and low oppose each other.
Fore and aft follow each other

—TAO TE CHING BY LAO-TZU.

This let me further add, that Nature knows
No stedfast station, but, or ebbs, or flows:
Ever in motion; she destroys her old,
And casts new figures in another mold.
Ev'n times are in perpetual flux, and run,
Like rivers from their fountain, rolling on,
For time, no more than streams, is at a stay;
The flying hour is ever on her way:

—OVID.
Metamorphoses, XV.

Chapter 13

ON CAUSE AND EFFECT,
CONDITIONALITY,
INTERDEPENDENCE

This being, that becomes.
From the arising of this, that arises.
This not being, that does not become.
From the ceasing of this, that ceases.

—Majjhima-Nikaya ii.32
The Middle-length
Discourses of the Buddha.

Whatsoever doth happen in the world, is, in the course of
nature, as usual and ordinary as a rose in the spring, and
fruit in summer. Of the same nature is sickness and death;
slander, and lying in wait, and whatsoever else ordinarily
doth unto fools use to be occasion either of joy or sorrow.
That, whatsoever it is, that comes after, doth always very
naturally, and as it were familiarly, follow upon that which
was before. For thou must consider the things of the world,
not as a loose independent number, consisting merely of
necessary events; but as a discreet connection of things
orderly and harmoniously disposed. There is then to be

seen in the things of the world, not a bare succession, but an admirable correspondence and affinity.

—MARCUS AURELIUS.
The Meditations of Marcus Aurelius.

.... for whatsoever a man soweth, that shall he also reap.

—GALATIANS 6:7. *KJV.*

Though the mills of God grind slowly,
Yet they grind exceeding small;
Though with patience he stands waiting,
With exactness grinds he all.

—HENRY WADSWORTH LONGFELLOW.
"Retribution."

Yet Clare's sharp questions must I shun
Must separate Constance from the nun
Oh! what a tangled web we weave
When first we practise to deceive!

—SIR WALTER SCOTT.
"Canto VI. Stanza 17." *Marmion.*

The life, the fortune, and the happiness of every one of us, and, more or less, of those who are connected with us, do depend upon our knowing something of the rules of a game infinitely more difficult and complicated than chess. It is a game which has been played for untold ages, every man and woman of us being one of the two players in a game of his or her own. The chessboard is the world, the pieces are the phenomena of the universe, the rules of the game are what we call the laws of Nature. The player on the other side is hidden from us. We know that his play is always fair, just and patient. But also we know, to our cost, that he never overlooks a mistake, or makes the smallest allowance for ignorance. To the man who plays well, the highest stakes are paid, with that sort of overflowing generosity with which the strong shows delight in strength. And one who plays ill is checkmated–without haste, but without remorse.

—THOMAS HUXLEY.
Aphorisms and Reflections.

Two principles in human nature reign;
Self-love to urge, and reason, to restrain;
Nor this a good, nor that a bad we call,
Each works its end, to move or govern all.

—ALEXANDER POPE.
Essay on Man.

The intuition of the moral sentiment is an insight of the perfection of the laws of the soul. These laws execute themselves. They are out of time, out of space, and not subject to circumstance. Thus; in the soul of man there is a justice whose retributions are instant and entire. He who does a good deed, is instantly ennobled. He who does a mean deed, is by the action itself contracted. He who puts off impurity, thereby puts on purity.

—Ralph Waldo Emerson.
The Divinity School Address.

We build our future, thought by thought,
For good or ill, yet know it not.
Yet, so the universe was wrought.
Thought is another name for fate;
Choose, then, thy destiny and wait.
For love brings love and hate brings hate.

—Henry Van Dyke.
"Thoughts Are Things."

Chapter 14

ON CHANCE, CHANGE, FATE, FORTUNE, PROVIDENCE

'Tis Providence alone secures
In every change both mine and yours:
Safety consists not in escape
From dangers of a frightful shape;
An earthquake may be bid to spare
The man that's strangled by a hair.
Fate steals along with silent tread,
Found oft'nest in what least we dread,
Frowns in the storm with angry brow,
But in the sunshine strikes the blow.

—WILLIAM COWPER.
"The Fable."

So use all that is called Fortune. Most men gamble with her, and gain all, and lose all, as her wheel rolls. But do thou leave as unlawful these winnings, and deal with Cause and Effect, the chancellors of God. In the Will work and acquire, and thou hast chained the wheel of Chance, and shalt sit hereafter out of fear from her rotations. A political victory, a rise of rents, the recovery of your sick, or the return of your absent friend, or some other favorable event, raises your spirits, and you think good days are preparing for you. Do not believe it. Nothing can bring you peace but yourself. Nothing can bring you peace but the triumph of principles.

—RALPH WALDO EMERSON.
"Self-Reliance." *Essays, First Series.*

Observe constantly that all things take place by change, and accustom thyself to consider that the nature of the Universe loves nothing so much as to change the things which are to make new things like them. For everything that exists is in a manner the seed of that which will be.

—MARCUS AURELIUS.
The Meditations of Marcus Aurelius.

'Now I would fain also reason with thee a little in Fortune's own words......

Wealth, honour, and all such things are placed under my control. My handmaidens know their mistress; with me they come, and at my going they depart. I might boldly affirm that if those things the loss of which thou lamentest had been thine, thou couldst never have lost them. Am I alone to be forbidden to do what I will with my own? Unrebuked, the skies now reveal the brightness of day, now shroud the daylight in the darkness of night; the year may now engarland the face of the earth with flowers and fruits, now disfigure it with storms and cold. The sea is permitted to invite with smooth and tranquil surface to-day, to-morrow to roughen with wave and storm. Shall man's insatiate greed bind *me* to a constancy foreign to my character? This is my art, this the game I never cease to play. I turn the wheel that spins. I delight to see the high come down and the low ascend. Mount up, if thou wilt, but only on condition that thou wilt not think it a hardship to come down when the rules of my game require it.

—BOETHIUS.
"Book II." *The Consolation of Philosophy of Boethius.*

In the day of prosperity be joyful, but in the day of adversity consider: God also hath set the one over against the other, to the end that man should find nothing after him.

—ECCLESIASTES 7:14. *KJV.*

All the best players do it. A fine retreat is as good as a gallant attack. Bring your exploits under cover when there are enough, or even when there are many of them. Luck long lasting was ever suspicious; interrupted seems safer, and is even sweeter to the taste for a little infusion of bitter-sweet. The higher the heap of luck, the greater the risk of a slip, and down comes all. Fortune pays you sometimes for the intensity of her favours by the shortness of their duration. She soon tires of carrying any one long on her shoulders.

—BALTASAR GRACIAN.
The Art of Worldly Wisdom.

I returned, and saw under the sun, that the race is not to the swift, nor the battle to the strong, neither yet bread to the wise, nor yet riches to men of understanding, nor yet favour to men of skill; but time and chance happeneth to them all.

—ECCLESIASTES 9:11. *KJV.*

We are as clouds that veil the midnight moon;
How restlessly they speed, and gleam, and quiver,
Streaking the darkness radiantly!—yet soon
Night closes round, and they are lost for ever:
Or like forgotten lyres, whose dissonant strings
Give various response to each varying blast,
To whose frail frame no second motion brings
One mood or modulation like the last.
We rest.—A dream has power to poison sleep;
We rise.—One wandering thought pollutes the day;
We feel, conceive or reason, laugh or weep;
Embrace fond woe, or cast our cares away:
It is the same!—For, be it joy or sorrow,
The path of its departure still is free:
Man's yesterday may ne'er be like his morrow;
Nought may endure but Mutability.

—PERCY BYSSHE SHELLEY.
"Mutability."

This let me further add, that Nature knows
No stedfast station, but, or ebbs, or flows:
Ever in motion; she destroys her old,
And casts new figures in another mold.
Ev'n times are in perpetual flux, and run,
Like rivers from their fountain, rolling on,
For time, no more than streams, is at a stay;
The flying hour is ever on her way:
And as the fountain still supplies her store,
The wave behind impels the wave before;
Thus in successive course the minutes run,
And urge their predecessor minutes on,
Till moving, ever new: for former things
Are set aside, like abdicated kings:
And every moment alters what is done,
And innovates some act, 'till then unknown.

—OVID.
Metamorphoses, XV.

So let us also win the way to victory in all our struggles,—for the reward is not a garland or a palm or a trumpeter who calls for silence at the proclamation of our names, but rather virtue, steadfastness of soul, and a peace that is won for all time, if fortune has once been utterly vanquished in any combat.

Meanwhile, hold fast to this thought, and grip it close: yield not to adversity; trust not to prosperity; keep before your eyes the full scope of Fortune's power, as if she would surely do whatever is in her power to do. That which has been long expected comes more gently.

—SENECA.
"Epistle LXXVIII.
On the Healing Power of the Mind."

Plato compared human life to a game at dice, wherein we ought to throw according to our requirements, and, having thrown, to make the best use of whatever turns up. It is not in our power indeed to determine what the throw will be, but it is our part, if we are wise, to accept in a right spirit whatever fortune sends.

—PLUTARCH.
"On Contentedness of Mind."

It cannot be denied, but outward accidents conduce much to fortune; favor, opportunity, death of others, occasion fitting virtue. But chiefly, the mould of a man's fortune is in his own hands.

And the most frequent of external causes is, that the folly of one man, is the fortune of another. For no man prospers so suddenly, as by others' errors.

Overt and apparent virtues, bring forth praise; but there be secret and hidden virtues, that bring forth fortune; certain deliveries of a man's self, which have no name. The Spanish name, desemboltura, partly expresseth them; when there be not stonds nor restiveness in a man's nature; but that the wheels of his mind, keep way with the wheels of his fortune.

Therefore if a man look sharply and attentively, he shall see
Fortune: for though she be blind, yet she is not invisible.

—FRANCIS BACON.
"Of Fortune." *Essays or Counsels Civil and Moral.*
From *The Works of Francis Bacon.*

When, in rosy chariot drawn,
Phœbus 'gins to light the dawn,
By his flaming beams assailed,
Every glimmering star is paled.
When the grove, by Zephyrs fed,
With rose-blossom blushes red;—
Doth rude Auster breathe thereon,
Bare it stands, its glory gone.
Smooth and tranquil lies the deep
While the winds are hushed in sleep.
Soon, when angry tempests lash,
Wild and high the billows dash.
Thus if Nature's changing face
Holds not still a moment's space,
Fleeting deem man's fortunes; deem
Bliss as transient as a dream.
One law only standeth fast:
Things created may not last.

—BOETHIUS.
"Song III, Book II."
The Consolation of Philosphy of Boethius.

Inasmuch as it teaches us, how we ought to conduct ourselves with respect to the gifts of fortune, or matters which are not in our power, and do not follow from our nature. For it shows us, that we should await and endure fortune's smiles or frowns with an equal mind, seeing that all things follow from the eternal decree of God by the same necessity, as it follows from the essence of a triangle, that the three angles are equal to two right angles.

—Benedict de Spinoza.
The Ethics.

One ship drives east and another drives west
With the self-same winds that blow;
'Tis the set of the sails
And not the gales
That tells them the way to go.
Like the winds of the sea are the winds of fate
As we voyage along through life;
'Tis the set of the soul
That decides its goal
And not the calm or the strife.

—Ella Wheeler Wilcox.
"The Winds of Fate."

It may well be that a man is at times horribly threshed by misfortunes, public and private: but the reckless flail of Fate, when it beats the rich sheaves, crushes only the straw; and the corn feels nothing of it and dances merrily on the floor, careless whether its way is to the mill or the furrow.

—JOHANN WOLFGANG VON GOETHE.
The Maxims and Reflections of Goethe.

What though Fortune should be niggardly to me in the distribution of good luck? I would make up the deficiency by my virtue. What though Fortune should condemn me to hard physical labour? I would find consolation from putting my mind at ease. What though Fortune should plunge me into adversity? I would get over difficulties by keeping to my convictions. When I am armed with such resolutions, what can Fortune do with me?

—HUNG YING-MING.
Musings of a Chinese Vegetarian.

If happy you would be tomorrow
Today must be a day of sorrow,
For Fortune's never tired of ranging
And Luck of all things loves place-changing:
Today's good luck, tomorrow bad;
Sorry today, tomorrow glad;
Take up, put down; now none, now all;
So spins teetotum, twirls the ball;

Lucky we bless kind Providence,
Unlucky, with no jot more sense
Upbraid the Author of all ill,
For man must be religious still,
And have his Oberon and his Puck,
That for his good, this for his ill luck.

—JAMES HENRY.
"Luck."

Chapter 15

ON POETRY

Here, your earth-born souls still speak
To mortals, of their little week;
Of their sorrows and delights;
Of their passions and their spites;
Of their glory and their shame;
What doth strengthen and what maim: -
Thus ye teach us, every day,
Wisdom, though fled far away.

Bards of Passion and of Mirth
Ye have left your souls on earth!
Ye have souls in heaven too,
Double-lived in regions new!

—JOHN KEATS.
"Ode (Bards of Passion and of Mirth)."

Poetry teaches the enormous force of a few words, and, in proportion to the inspiration, checks loquacity. It requires that splendor of expression which carries with it the proof of great thoughts. Great thoughts insure musical expressions. Every word should be the right word. The poets are they who see that spiritual is greater than any material force, that thoughts rule the world.

—Ralph Waldo Emerson.
"Preface." *Parnassus: An Anthology of Poetry.*

The poet's eye, in a fine frenzy rolling,
Doth glance from heaven to earth, from earth to heaven;
And as imagination bodies forth
The forms of things unknown, the poet's pen
Turns them to shapes, and gives to airy nothing
A local habitation and a name.

—William Shakespeare.
A Midsummer Night's Dream. Act 5. Scene 1.

Poetry is the language of the imagination and the passions. It relates to whatever gives immediate pleasure or pain to the human mind.

It is not a mere frivolous accomplishment (as some persons have been led to imagine) the trifling amusement of a few idle readers or leisure hours - it has been the study and delight of mankind in all ages. Many people suppose that poetry is something to be found only in books, contained in lines of ten syllables, with like endings: but wherever there is a sense of beauty, or power, or harmony, as in the motion of a wave of the sea, in the growth of a flower that 'spreads its sweet leaves to the air, and dedicates its beauty to the sun',—there is poetry, in its birth.

—William Hazlitt.
"On Poetry in General."

Come, read to me some poem,
Some simple and heartfelt lay,
That shall soothe this restless feeling,
And banish the thoughts of day.
Not from the grand old masters,
Not from the bards sublime,
Whose distant footsteps echo
Through the corridors of Time.
For, like strains of martial music,
Their mighty thoughts suggest
Life's endless toil and endeavor;
And to-night I long for rest.
Read from some humbler poet,
Whose songs gushed from his heart,
As showers from the clouds of summer,
Or tears from the eyelids start;
Who, through long days of labor,
And nights devoid of ease,
Still heard in his soul the music
Of wonderful melodies.
Such songs have power to quiet
The restless pulse of care,
And come like the benediction
That follows after prayer.
Then read from the treasured volume
The poem of thy choice,
And lend to the rhyme of the poet
The beauty of thy voice.
And the night shall be filled with music
And the cares that infest the day,
Shall fold their tents, like the Arabs,

And as silently steal away.

—HENRY WADSWORTH LONGFELLOW.
"The Day Is Done."

Therefore we value the poet. All the argument and all the wisdom is not in the encyclopaedia, or the treatise on metaphysics, or the Body of Divinity, but in the sonnet or the play. In my daily work I incline to repeat my old steps, and do not believe in remedial force, in the power of change and reform. But some Petrarch or Ariosto, filled with the new wine of his imagination, writes me an ode or a brisk romance, full of daring thought and action. He smites and arouses me with his shrill tones, breaks up my whole chain of habits, and I open my eye on my own possibilities. He claps wings to the sides of all the solid old lumber of the world, and I am capable once more of choosing a straight path in theory and practice.

—RALPH WALDO EMERSON.
"Circles." *Essays, First Series.*

They please me not—these solemn songs
That hint of sermons covered up.
'T is true the world should heed its wrongs,
But in a poem let me sup,
Not simples brewed to cure or ease
Humanity's confessed disease,
But the spirit-wine of a singing line,
Or a dew-drop in a honey cup!

—PAUL LAURENCE DUNBAR.
"A Choice."

The advancing man discovers how deep a property he has in literature,—in all fable as well as in all history. He finds that the poet was no odd fellow who described strange and impossible situations, but that universal man wrote by his pen a confession true for one and true for all.

—Ralph Waldo Emerson.
"History." *Essays, First Series.*

Imaginative poetry produces a far greater mental strain than novels. It produces probably the severest strain of any form of literature. It is the highest form of literature. It yields the highest form of pleasure, and teaches the highest form of wisdom. In a word, there is nothing to compare with it.

—Arnold Bennett.
How to Live on Twenty-four Hours a Day.

A Song is but a little thing,
And yet what joy it is to sing!
In hours of toil it gives me zest,
And when at eve I long for rest;
When cows come home along the bars,
And in the fold I hear the bell,
As Night, the shepherd, herds his stars,
I sing my song, and all is well.
My days are never days of ease;
I till my ground and prune my trees.
When ripened gold is all the plain,
I put my sickle to the grain.

I labor hard, and toil and sweat,
While others dream within the dell;
But even while my brow is wet,
I sing my song, and all is well.
Sometimes the sun, unkindly hot,
My garden makes a desert spot;
Sometimes a blight upon the tree
Takes all my fruit away from me;
And then with throes of bitter pain
Rebellious passions rise and swell;
But - life is more than fruit or grain,
And so I sing, and all is well.

—PAUL LAURENCE DUNBAR.
"A Poet and his Song."

I cannot open my eyes without admiring the art that shines throughout all nature; the least cast suffices to make me perceive the Hand that makes everything. Nay, what is called the art of men is but a faint imitation of the great art called the laws of Nature, and which the impious did not blush to call blind chance. Is it therefore a wonder that poets animated the whole universe, bestowed wings upon the winds, and arrows on the sun, and described great rivers impetuously running to precipitate themselves into the sea, and trees shooting up to heaven to repel the rays of the sun by their thick shades? These images and figures have also been received in the language of the vulgar, so natural it is for men to be sensible of the wonderful art that fills all nature. Poetry did only ascribe to inanimate creatures the art and design of the Creator, who does everything in them. From the figurative language of the poets those notions passed into the theology of the heathens, whose divines were the poets. They supposed an art, a power, or a wisdom, which they called *numen*, in creatures the most destitute of understanding. With them great rivers were gods; and springs, naiads. Woods and mountains had their particular deities; flowers had their Flora; and fruits, Pomona. After all, the more a man contemplates Nature, the more he discovers in it an inexhaustible stock of wisdom, which is, as it were, the soul of the universe.

—Francois de Salignac de La Mothe-Fénelon.
A Demonstration of the Existence and Attributes of God.

Poet, a truce to your song!
Have you heard the heart sing?
Like a brook among trees,
Like the humming of bees,
Like the ripple of wine:
Had you heard, would you stay
Blowing bubbles so long?
You have ears for the spheres—
Have you heard the heart sing?
Have you loved the good books of the world,—
And written none?
Have you loved the great poet,—
And burnt your little rhyme?
'O be my friend, and teach me to be thine.'
By many hands the work of God is done,
Swart toil, pale thought, flushed dream, he spurneth none:

Yea! and the weaver of a little rhyme
Is seen his worker in his own full time.

—RICHARD LE GALLIENNE.
"Inscriptions."

The least activity of the intellectual powers redeems us in a degree from the conditions of time. In sickness, in languor, give us a strain of poetry or a profound sentence, and we are refreshed; or produce a volume of Plato or Shakespeare, or remind us of their names, and instantly we come into a feeling of longevity. See how the deep divine thought reduces centuries and millenniums and makes itself present through all ages.

—RALPH WALDO EMERSON.
"The Over-Soul." *Essays, First Series.*

The Poet is a heroic figure belonging to all ages; whom all ages possess, when once he is produced, whom the newest age as the oldest may produce;—and will produce, always when Nature pleases. Let Nature send a Hero-soul; in no age is it other than possible that he may be shaped into a Poet.

Poet and Prophet differ greatly in our loose modern notions of them. In some old languages, again, the titles are synonymous; Vates means both Prophet and Poet: and indeed at all times, Prophet and Poet, well understood, have much kindred of meaning. Fundamentally indeed they are still the same; in this most important respect especially, that they have penetrated both of them into the sacred mystery of the Universe; what Goethe calls "the open secret." "Which is the great secret?" asks one.—"The open secret,"—open to all, seen by almost none! That divine mystery, which lies everywhere in all Beings, "the Divine Idea of the World, that which lies at the bottom of Appearance," as Fichte styles it; of which all Appearance, from the starry sky to the grass of the field, but especially the Appearance of Man and his work, is but the vesture, the embodiment that renders it visible. This divine mystery is in all times and in all places; veritably is.

—Thomas Carlyle.
On Heroes, Hero-worship and the Heroic in History.

Po, the poet unrivaled,
In fancy's realm, you soar alone.
Yours is the delicacy of Yui,
And Pao's rare virility.
Now on the north of the Wei River
I see the trees under the vernal sky
While you wander beneath the sunset clouds
Far down in Chiang-tung.
When shall we by a cask of wine once more
Argue minutely on versification?

—Tu Fu.
"To Li Po on a Spring Day."

Hail to thee, blithe Spirit!
Bird thou never wert,
That from Heaven, or near it,
Pourest thy full heart
In profuse strains of unpremeditated art.

Like a Poet hidden
In the light of thought,
Singing hymns unbidden,
Till the world is wrought
To sympathy with hopes and fears it heeded not:

Better than all measures
Of delightful sound,
Better than all treasures
That in books are found,
Thy skill to poet were, thou scorner of the ground!

Teach me half the gladness
That thy brain must know,
Such harmonious madness
From my lips would flow
The world should listen then, as I am listening now.

—PERCY BYSSHE SHELLEY.
"To a Skylark."

I walked with poets in my youth,
Because the world they drew
Was beautiful and glorious
Beyond the world I knew.
The poets are my comrades still,

But dearer than in youth,
For now I know that they alone
Picture the world of truth.

—WILLIAM ROSCOE THAYER.
"Envoi."

Chapter 16

ON WORK

But he who, with strong body serving mind,
Gives up his mortal powers to worthy work,
Not seeking gain, Arjuna! such an one
Is honourable. Do thine allotted task!
Work is more excellent than idleness;
The body's life proceeds not, lacking work.
There is a task of holiness to do,
Unlike world-binding toil, which bindeth not
The faithful soul; such earthly duty do
Free from desire, and thou shalt well perform
Thy heavenly purpose.

—THE BHAGAVAD-GITA.

'Work,' it saith to man, 'in every hour, paid or unpaid, see only that thou work, and thou canst not escape the reward: whether thy work be fine or coarse, planting corn, or writing epics, so only it be honest work, done to thine own approbation, it shall earn a reward to the senses as well as to the thought: no matter, how often defeated, you are born to victory. The reward of a thing well done, is to have done it.'

—RALPH WALDO EMERSON.
"New England Reformers."

Whatsoever thy hand findeth to do, do it with thy might.

—Ecclesiastes 9:10. *KJV.*

Then a ploughman said, "Speak to us of Work."
And he answered, saying:
You work that you may keep pace with the earth and the soul of the earth.
For to be idle is to become a stranger unto the seasons, and to step out of life's procession, that marches in majesty and proud submission towards the infinite.

—Kahlil Gibran.
The Prophet.

Work indeed, and hard work, if only it is in moderation, is in itself a rich source of happiness. We all know how quickly time passes when we are well employed, while the moments hang heavily on the hands of the idle. Occupation drives away care and all the small troubles of life. The busy man has no time to brood or to fret.

—Sir John Lubbock.
"Labor and Rest." *The Pleasures of Life.*

Whoso performeth—diligent, content—
The work allotted him, whate'er it be,
Lays hold of perfectness! Hear how a man
Findeth perfection, being so content:

On the Nature of Things   119

He findeth it through worship—wrought by work—
Of Him that is the Source of all which lives,
Of HIM by Whom the universe was stretched.

—THE BHAGAVAD-GITA.

The trivial round, the common task,
will furnish all we ought to ask:
room to deny ourselves; a road
to bring us daily nearer God.

—JOHN KEBLE.
"Morning."

Under a spreading chestnut-tree
The village smithy stands;
The smith, a mighty man is he,
With large and sinewy hands;
And the muscles of his brawny arms
Are strong as iron bands.

Toiling, - rejoicing, - sorrowing,
Onward through life he goes;
Each morning sees some task begin,
Each evening sees it close
Something attempted, something done,
Has earned a night's repose.
Thanks, thanks to thee, my worthy friend,
For the lesson thou hast taught!
Thus at the flaming forge of life

Our fortunes must be wrought;
Thus on its sounding anvil shaped
Each burning deed and thought.

—Henry Wadsworth Longfellow.
"The Village Blacksmith."

"I have only twenty acres," replied the old man; "I and my children cultivate them; our labour preserves us from three great evils – weariness, vice, and want."

—Voltaire.
Candide.

Let me but do my work from day to day,
In field or forest, at the desk or loom,
In roaring market-place or tranquil room;
Let me but find it in my heart to say,
When vagrant wishes beckon me astray,
This is my work; my blessing, not my doom;
Of all who live, I am the one by whom
"This work can best be done in the right way."
Then shall I see it not too great, nor small,
To suit my spirit and to prove my powers;
Then shall I cheerful greet the labouring hours,
And cheerful turn, when the long shadows fall
At eventide, to play and love and rest,
Because I know for me my work is best.

—Henry Van Dyke.
"Work."

That is what is meant by working for duty. It makes all life comparatively easy. It makes it calm, strong, impartial, and undaunted; for the man does not cling to anything he does. When he has done it, he has no more concern with it. Let it go for success or failure as the world counts them, for he knows the Life within is ever going onwards to its goal. And it is the secret of peace in work, because those who work for success are always troubled, always anxious, always counting their forces, reckoning their chances and possibilities; but the man who cares nothing for success but only for duty, he works with the strength of divinity, and his aim is always sure.

—ANNIE BESANT.
The Meaning and Method of the Spiritual Life.

He, when his morning task is done,
Can slumber in the noontide sun
And hie him home, at evening's close,
To sweet repast and calm repose.
From toil he wins his spirits light,
From busy day the peaceful night;
Rich, from the very want of wealth,
In heaven's best treasures, peace and health."

—THOMAS GRAY.
"Ode on the Pleasure Arising from Vicissitude."

For there is a perennial nobleness, and even sacredness, in Work. Were he never so benighted, forgetful of his high calling, there is always hope in a man that actually and earnestly works: in Idleness alone is there perpetual despair. Work, never so Mammonish, mean, is in communication with Nature; the real desire to get Work done will itself lead one more and more to truth, to Nature's appointments and regulations, which are truth. The latest Gospel in this world is, Know thy work and do it.

Blessed is he who has found his work; let him ask no other blessedness. He has a work, a life-purpose; he has found it, and will follow it! How, as a free-flowing channel, dug and torn by noble force through the sour mud-swamp of one's existence, like an ever-deepening river there, it runs and flows.

—Thomas Carlyle.
"Chapter 11: Labour." *Past and Present.*

神通並妙用 Miraculous power and marvelous activity–
運水及槃柴 Drawing water and hewing wood!

—P'ang Yün.

Chapter 17

On Time

When I do count the clock that tells the time,
And see the brave day sunk in hideous night;
When I behold the violet past prime,
And sable curls all silver'd o'er with white;
When lofty trees I see barren of leaves
Which erst from heat did canopy the herd,
And summer's green all girded up in sheaves
Borne on the bier with white and bristly beard,
Then of thy beauty do I question make,
That thou among the wastes of time must go,
Since sweets and beauties do themselves forsake
And die as fast as they see others grow;
And nothing 'gainst Time's scythe can make defence
Save breed, to brave him when he takes thee hence.

—WILLIAM SHAKESPEARE.
"Sonnet XII."

Dost thou love life? Then do not squander time; for that's
the stuff life is made of.

—BENJAMIN FRANKLIN.
Poor Richard's Almanack.

All other good gifts depend on time for their value. What are friends, books, or health, the interest of travel or the delights of home, if we have not time for their enjoyment? Time is often said to be money, but it is more-it is life; and yet many who would cling desperately to life, think nothing of wasting time.

—Sir John Lubbock.
"The Value of Time." *The Pleasures of Life.*

Time is
Too Slow for those who Wait,
Too Swift for those who Fear,
Too Long for those who Grieve,
Too Short for those who Rejoice;
But for those who Love,
Time is not.

—Henry Van Dyke.
"Katrina's Sun-Dial."

To everything there is a season,
a time for every purpose under the sun.
a time to be born and a time to die;
a time to plant and a time to pluck up that which is planted;
a time to kill and a time to heal...
a time to weep and a time to laugh;
a time to mourn and a time to dance...
a time to embrace and a time to refrain from embracing;
a time to lose and a time to seek;

a time to rend and a time to sew;
a time to keep silent and a time to speak;
a time to love and a time to hate;
a time for war and a time for peace.

—ECCLESIASTES 3:1-8. *KJV.*

Ask what Time is, it is nothing else but something of eternal duration become finite, measurable and transitory.

—WILLIAM LAW.
The Works of the Reverend William Law, M.A.

It is not that we have a short space of time, but that we waste much of it. Life is long enough, and it has been given in sufficiently generous measure to allow the accomplishment of the very greatest things if the whole of it is well invested. But when it is squandered in luxury and carelessness, when it is devoted to no good end, forced at last by the ultimate necessity we perceive that it has passed away before we were aware that it was passing. So it is—the life we receive is not short, but we make it so, nor do we have any lack of it, but are wasteful of it. Just as great and princely wealth is scattered in a moment when it comes into the hands of a bad owner, while wealth however limited, if it is entrusted to a good guardian, increases by use, so our life is amply long for him who orders it properly.

—LUCIUS ANNAEUS SENECA.
On the Shortness of Life.

"I wasted time, and now doth time waste me."

—WILLIAM SHAKESPEARE.
Richard II. Act 5, Scene 5.

Hours have wings and fly up to the author of time and carry news of our usage. All our prayers cannot entreat one of them either to return or slacken its pace. The misspents of every minute are a new record against us in heaven. Sure if we thought thus we would dismiss them with better reports, and not suffer them to fly away empty, or laden with dangerous intelligence. How happy is it when they carry up not only the message but the fruits of good, and stay with the Ancient of Days to speak for us before his glorious throne.

—JOHN MILTON.
The World's Laconics:
Or The Best Thoughts of the Best Authors.

'Tis greatly wise to talk with our past hours,
And ask them what report they bore to heaven.

—EDWARD YOUNG.
Night-Thoughts on Life, Death, and Immortality.

The water you touch in a river is the last of that which has passed, and the first of that which is coming. Thus it is with time present. Life if well spent, is long.

—*THE NOTEBOOKS OF LEONARDO DA VINCI.*

On the Nature of Things   127

We are not slaves of Time, save as we bow to his imperious tyranny, and let him bind over our eyes his bandages of birth and death. We are always ourselves, and can pace steadfastly onwards through the changing lights and shadows cast by his magic lantern on the life he cannot age. Why are the Gods figured as ever-young, save to remind us that the true life lives untouched by Time? We borrow some of the strength and calm of Eternity when we try to live in it, escaping from the meshes of the great Enchanter.

—ANNIE BESANT.
"Some Difficulties of the Inner Life."

The least activity of the intellectual powers redeems us in a degree from the conditions of time. In sickness, in languor, give us a strain of poetry or a profound sentence, and we are refreshed; or produce a volume of Plato or Shakespeare, or remind us of their names, and instantly we come into a feeling of longevity. See how the deep divine thought reduces centuries and millenniums and makes itself present through all ages. Is the teaching of Christ less effective now than it was when first his mouth was opened?

—RALPH WALDO EMERSON.
"The Over-Soul." *Essays, First Series.*

There is a time for everything in our lives; but the maxim that governs every moment, is, that there should be none useless.

For we misemploy our time, not only when we do wrong or do nothing, but also when we do something else than what was incumbent on us at the moment, even though it may be the means of good.

Our leisure hours are ordinarily the sweetest and pleasantest for ourselves; we can never employ them better than in refreshing our spiritual strength.

—Francois de Salignac de La Mothe- Fénelon.
Spiritual Progress.

Philosophers have explained space. They have not explained time. It is the inexplicable raw material of everything. With it, all is possible; without it, nothing. The supply of time is truly a daily miracle, an affair genuinely astonishing when one examines it. You wake up in the morning, and lo! your purse is magically filled with twenty-four hours of the unmanufactured tissue of the universe of your life! It is yours. It is the most precious of possessions. A highly singular commodity, showered upon you in a manner as singular as the commodity itself!

—Arnold Bennett.
How to Live on Twenty-four Hours a Day.

Time, whose tooth gnaws away everything else, is powerless against truth.

—Thomas H. Huxley.
Aphorisms and Reflections.

Time, which gnaws and diminisheth all things else, augments and increaseth benefits; because a noble action of liberality, done to a man of reason, doth grow continually by his generous thinking of it and remembering it.

—François Rabelais.
Gargantua.

So here hath been dawning
Another blue Day:
Think wilt thou let it
Slip useless away.
Out of Eternity
This new Day is born;
Into Eternity,
At night, will return.
Behold it aforetime
No eye ever did:
So soon it forever
From all eyes is hid.
Here hath been dawning
Another blue Day:
Think wilt thou let it
Slip useless away.

—Thomas Carlyle.
"Today."

Time must elapse between sowing and harvest, nay even in the growth of such wild grass as the holy Kusa and the like; reflection on the Self ripens into self-realization by degrees, and in course of time.

—PANCHADASI.
*The Spirit of the Upanishads
(or the Aphorisms of the Wise).*

Avoid the company of drunkards and busybodies, and all such as are apt to talk much to little purpose; for no man can be provident of his time that is not prudent in the choice of his company; and if one of the speakers be vain, tedious, and trifling, he that hears, and he that answers in the discourse, are equal losers of their time.

—JEREMY TAYLOR. *The Rules and Exercises of Holy Living.*

*Whether we wake or we sleep,
Whether we carol or weep,
The Sun with his Planets in chime,
Marketh the going of Time.
But Time, in a still better trim,
Marketh the going of him:
One link in an infinite chain,
Is this turning the hour-glass again!*

*And yet, after all, what is Time?
Renowned in Reason, and Rhyme,
A Phantom, a Name, a Notion,*

That measures Duration or Motion?
Or but an apt term in the lease
Of Beings, who know they must cease?
The hand utters more than the brain,
When turning the hour-glass again!

—EDWARD FITZGERALD.
"Chronomoros." *Letters and Literary*
Remains of Edward FitzGerald.

With constant motion as the moments glide.
Behold in running life the rolling tide!
For none can stem by art, or stop by pow'r,
The flowing ocean, or the fleeting hour:
But wave by wave pursued arrives on shore,
And each impell'd behind impels before:
So time on time revolving we descry;
So minutes follow, and so minutes fly.

—OVID.
Metamorphoses, XV.

On drives the road - another mile! and still
Time's horses gallop down the lessening hill
O why such haste, with nothing at the end!
Fain are we all, grim driver, to descend
And stretch with lingering feet the little way
That yet is ours - O stop thy horses, pray!
Yet, sister dear, if we indeed had grace
To win from Time one lasting halting-place,

Which out of all life's valleys would we choose,
And, choosing—which with willingness would lose?
Would we as children be content to stay,
Because the children are as birds all day;
Or would we still as youngling lovers kiss,
Fearing the ardours of the greater bliss?
The maid be still a maid and never know
Why mothers love their little blossoms so
Or can the mother be content her bud
Shall never open out of babyhood?
Ah yes, Time flies because we fain would fly,
It is such ardent souls as you and I,
Greedy of living, give his wings to him—
And now we grumble that he uses them!

—RICHARD LE GALLIENNE.
"Time Flies."

Yet no one will bring back the years, no one will bestow you
once more on yourself. Life will follow the path it started
upon, and will neither reverse nor check its course; it will
make no noise, it will not remind you of its swiftness. Silent
it will glide on; it will not prolong itself at the command
of a king, or at the applause of the populace. Just as it was
started on its first day, so it will run; nowhere will it turn
aside, nowhere will it delay.

—LUCIUS ANNAEUS SENECA.
On the Shortness of Life.

"The strongest of all warriors are these two—Time and Patience."

—LEO TOLSTOY.
War and Peace.

Time's crutch effects more than the iron club of Hercules. God Himself chasteneth not with a rod but with time. He spake a great word who said, "Time and I against any two."

—BALTASAR GRACIAN.
The Art of Worldly Wisdom.

Though heaven and earth are eternal, we are not born again. Human life is short at the longest; nothing flies more swiftly than time. Therefore, those who have been fortunate enough to see the light should make the most of life; they should consider how miserable it is to whistle their days away.

—HUNG YING-MING.
Musings of a Chinese Vegetarian.

Life itself is a mixture of power and form, and will not bear the least excess of either. To finish the moment, to find the journey's end in every step of the road, to live the greatest number of good hours, is wisdom. It is not the part of men, but of fanatics, or of mathematicians, if you will, to say, that, the shortness of life considered, it is not worth caring whether for so short a duration we were sprawling in want, or sitting high. Since our office is with moments, let us husband them. Five minutes of today are worth as much to me, as five minutes in the next millennium.

—Ralph Waldo Emerson.
"Experience." *Essays, Second Series.*

Chapter 18

On the Music, Art, Dance of Nature and Life

Dance, my heart! dance to-day with joy.
The strains of love fill the days and the nights with music, and
the world is listening to its melodies:
Mad with joy, life and death dance to the rhythm of this music.
The hills and the sea and the earth dance. The world of man
dances in laughter and tears.
Why put on the robe of the monk, and live aloof from the world in
lonely pride?
Behold! my heart dances in the delight of a hundred arts; and
the Creator is well pleased.

—KABIR.
Songs of Kabir.

Poetry, therefore, we will call musical Thought. The Poet is he who thinks in that manner. At bottom, it turns still on power of intellect; it is a man's sincerity and depth of vision that makes him a Poet. See deep enough, and you see musically; the heart of Nature being everywhere music, if you can only reach it.

—THOMAS CARLYLE.
On Heroes, Hero-worship and the Heroic in History.

Speaking to yourselves in psalms and hymns and spiritual songs, singing and making melody in your heart to the Lord.

—EPHESIANS: 5:19. *KJV.*

Read from some humbler poet,
Whose songs gushed from his heart,
As showers from the clouds of summer,
Or tears from the eyelids start;
Who, through long days of labor,
And nights devoid of ease,
Still heard in his soul the music
Of wonderful melodies.
Such songs have power to quiet
The restless pulse of care,
And come like the benediction
That follows after prayer.

—HENRY WADSWORTH LONGFELLOW.
"The Day Is Done."

Nature! We are surrounded by her and locked in her clasp: powerless to leave her, and powerless to come closer to her. Unasked and unwarned she takes us up into the whirl of her dance, and hurries on with us till we are weary and fall from her arms.

—JOHANN WOLFGANG VON GOETHE.
The Maxims and Reflections of Goethe.

The song of Nature is forever,
Her joyous voices falter never;
On hill and valley, near and far,
Attendant her musicians are.
From waterbrook or forest tree
For aye comes gentle melody;
The very air is music blent,
A universal instrument.
When hushed are bird and brook and wind,
Then silence will some measure find,
Still sweeter; as a memory
Is sweeter than the things that be.

—JOHN VANCE CHENEY.
"The Music of Nature."

There lives a Master in the hearts of men
Maketh their deeds, by subtle pulling—strings,
Dance to what tune HE will. With all thy soul
Trust Him, and take Him for thy succour, Prince!
So—only so, Arjuna!—shalt thou gain—
By grace of Him—the uttermost repose,
The Eternal Place!

—THE BHAGAVAD-GITA.

The flute of the Infinite is played without ceasing, and its
sound is love:
When love renounces all limits, it reaches truth.
How widely the fragrance spreads! It has no end, nothing

stands in its way.
The form of this melody is bright like a million suns:
incomparably sounds the vina, the vina of the notes of
truth.

—KABIR.
Songs of Kabir.

A SONG is but a little thing,
And yet what joy it is to sing!
In hours of toil it gives me zest,
And when at eve I long for rest;
When cows come home along the bars,
And in the fold I hear the bell,
As Night, the shepherd, herds his stars,
I sing my song, and all is well.

My days are never days of ease;
I till my ground and prune my trees.
When ripened gold is all the plain,
I put my sickle to the grain.
I labor hard, and toil and sweat,
While others dream within the dell;
But even while my brow is wet,
I sing my song, and all is well.
Sometimes the sun, unkindly hot,
My garden makes a desert spot;
Sometimes a blight upon the tree
Takes all my fruit away from me;
And then with throes of bitter pain
Rebellious passions rise and swell;

But - life is more than fruit or grain,
And so I sing, and all is well.

—Paul Laurence Dunbar.
"A Poet and his Song."

We may compare existence to raw material. What it is, matters less than what is made of it, as the value of a work of art lies in the flowering of the workman's skill. We bring into the world with us different gifts: one has received gold, another granite, a third marble, most of us wood or clay. Our task is to fashion these substances. Everyone knows that the most precious material may be spoiled, and he knows, too, that out of the least costly an immortal work may be shaped. Art is the realization of a permanent idea in an ephemeral form.

—Charles Wagner.
The Simple Life.

In fact, unity, agreement is always silent, or soft-voiced; it is only discord that loudly proclaims itself. So long as the several elements of Life, all fitly adjusted, can pour forth their movement like harmonious tuned strings, it is a melody and unison; Life, from its mysterious fountains, flows out as in celestial music and diapason,—which also, like that other music of the spheres, even because it is perennial and complete, without interruption and without imperfection, might be fabled to escape the ear.

—Thomas Carlyle. "Characteristics."

If a man does not keep pace with his companions, perhaps it is because he hears a different drummer. Let him step to the music which he hears, however measured or far away.

—HENRY DAVID THOREAU.
Walden.

How sour sweet music is when time is broke and no proportion kept! So is it in the music of men's lives.

—WILLIAM SHAKESPEARE.
Richard II. Act 5, Scene 5.

ON the dusty earth-drum
Beats the falling rain;
Now a whispered murmur,
Now a louder strain.
Slender, silvery drumsticks,
On an ancient drum,
Beat the mellow music
Bidding life to come.
Chords of earth awakened,
Notes of greening spring,
Rise and fall triumphant
Over every thing.
Slender, silvery drumsticks
Beat the long tattoo—
God, the Great Musician,
Calling life anew.

—JOSEPH S. Cotter, Jr.
"Rain Music."

There are in this loud stunning tide
Of human care and crime,
With whom the melodies abide
Of th' everlasting chime;
Who carry music in their heart
Through dusky lane and wrangling mart,
Plying their daily task with busier feet,
Because their secret souls a holy strain repeat.

—JOHN KEBLE.
"St. Matthew."

A musical thought is one spoken by a mind that has penetrated into the inmost heart of the thing; detected the inmost mystery of it, namely the melody that lies hidden in it; the inward harmony of coherence which is its soul, whereby it exists, and has a right to be, here in this world. All inmost things, we may say, are melodious; naturally utter themselves in Song. The meaning of Song goes deep. Who is there that, in logical words, can express the effect music has on us? A kind of inarticulate unfathomable speech, which leads us to the edge of the Infinite, and lets us for moments gaze into that!

—THOMAS CARLYLE.
On Heroes, Hero-worship and the Heroic in History.

It is a great mortification to the vanity of man, that his utmost art and industry can never equal the meanest of Nature's productions, either for beauty or value. Art is only the under-workman, and is employed to give a few strokes of embellishment to those pieces, which come from the hand of the master. Some of the drapery may be of his drawing; but he is not allowed to touch the principal figure. Art may make a suit of clothes: but nature must produce a man.

—DAVID HUME.
"Essay 15: The Epicurean."
Essays Moral, Political, and Literary, Volume 1.

Part Three

ON CHARACTER, CONDUCT, VIRTUES

Chapter 19

ON MODERATION, THE MIDDLE WAY, THE GOLDEN MEAN

But for earthly need Religion is not his who too much fasts
Or too much feasts, nor his who sleeps away
An idle mind; nor his who wears to waste
His strength in vigils. Nay, Arjuna! call
That the true piety which most removes
Earth-aches and ills, where one is moderate
In eating and in resting, and in sport;
Measured in wish and act; sleeping betimes,
Waking betimes for duty.

—THE BHAGAVAD-GITA.

A sage once reduced all virtue to the golden mean. Push right to the extreme and it becomes wrong: press all the juice from an orange and it becomes bitter. Even in enjoyment never go to extremes. Thought too subtle is dull.

—BALTASAR GRACIAN.
The Art of Wordly Wisdom.

Licinius, trust a seaman's lore:
Steer not too boldly to the deep,
Nor, fearing storms, by treacherous shore
Too closely creep.

Who makes the golden mean his guide,
Shuns miser's cabin, foul and dark,
Shuns gilded roofs, where pomp and pride
Are envy's mark.

With fiercer blasts the pine's dim height
Is rock'd; proud towers with heavier fall
Crash to the ground; and thunders smite
The mountains tall.

In sadness hope, in gladness fear
'Gainst coming change will fortify
Your breast. The storms that Jupiter
Sweeps o'er the sky

He chases. Why should rain today
Bring rain tomorrow? Python's foe
Is pleased sometimes his lyre to play,
Nor bends his bow.

Be brave in trouble; meet distress
With dauntless front; but when the gale
Too prosperous blows, be wise no less,
And shorten sail.

—Horace.
"Odes 2.10." *The Odes and Carmen*
Saeculare of Horace.

For, as the strings of the bow and lyre are alternately tightened and relaxed, so is it with the order of the world; in human affairs there is nothing pure and without alloy. But as in music there are high and low notes, and in grammar vowels and mutes, but neither the musician nor grammarian decline to use either kinds, but know how to blend and employ them both for their purpose, so in human affairs which are balanced one against another.

—PLUTARCH.
"On Contentedness of Mind."

I am neither pious nor ungodly, I live neither by law nor by sense,
I am neither a speaker nor hearer, I am neither a servant nor master, I am neither bond nor free,
I am neither detached nor attached.
I am far from none: I am near to none.
I shall go neither to hell nor to heaven.
I do all works; yet I am apart from all works.
Few comprehend my meaning: he who can comprehend it, he sits unmoved.
Kabîr seeks neither to establish nor to destroy.

—KABIR.
Songs of Kabir.

The man within the golden mean
Who can his boldest wish contain,
Securely views the ruin'd cell,
Where sordid want and sorrow dwell;
And in himself serenely great,
Declines an envied room of state.

—HORACE.
"Ode 4.10." *The Odes.*

Among many parallels which men of imagination have drawn between the natural and moral state of the world, it has been observed that happiness, as well as virtue, consists in mediocrity; that to avoid every extreme is necessary, even to him who has no other care than to pass through the present state with ease and safety; and that the middle path is the road of security, on either side of which are not only the pitfalls of vice, but the precipices of ruin.

Thus the maxim of Cleobulus the Lindian, Mediocrity is best, has been long considered as an universal principle, extended through the whole compass of life and nature. The experience of every age seems to have given it new confirmation, and to shew that nothing, however specious or alluring, is pursued with propriety, or enjoyed with safety, beyond certain limits.

—SAMUEL JOHNSON.
"No. 38." *The Rambler.*

The middle region of our being is the temperate zone. We may climb into the thin and cold realm of pure geometry and lifeless science, or sink into that of sensation. Between these extremes is the equator of life, of thought, of spirit, of poetry,—a narrow belt.

—RALPH WALDO EMERSON.
"Experience." *Essays, Second Series.*

If you be moderate in doing anything, the Creator cannot be envious of you, nor can gods and evil spirits do harm to you. Never seek fullness in all your endeavors, for such ambition will surely give rise to either internal or external troubles.

—HUNG YING-MING.
Musings of a Chinese Vegetarian.

Let us then take our compass; we are something, and we are not everything. The nature of our existence hides from us the knowledge of first beginnings which are born of the Nothing; and the littleness of our being conceals from us the sight of the Infinite.

Our intellect holds the same position in the world of thought as our body occupies in the expanse of nature.

Limited as we are in every way, this state which holds the mean between two extremes is present in all our impotence. Our senses perceive no extreme. Too much sound deafens us; too much light dazzles us; too great distance or proximity hinders our view. Too great length and too great brevity of discourse tend to obscurity; too much truth is paralysing (I know some who cannot understand that to take four from nothing leaves nothing). First principles are too self-evident for us; too much pleasure disagrees with us. Too many concords are annoying in music; too many benefits irritate us; we wish to have the wherewithal to over-pay our debts. We feel neither extreme heat nor extreme cold. Excessive qualities are prejudicial to us and not perceptible by the senses; we do not feel but suffer them. Extreme youth and extreme age hinder the mind, as also too much and too little education. In short, extremes are for us as though they were not, and we are not within their notice. They escape us, or we them.

—BLAISE PASCAL.
Pensées (Thoughts).

Chapter 20

ON GRATITUDE, THANKFULNESS

When thou hast thanked thy God
For every blessing sent,
What time will then remain
For murmurs or lament.

—RICHARD CHENEVIX TRENCH.
"A Century of Couplets."
Sabbation; Honor Neale; and Other Poems.

In everything give thanks.

—1 THESSALONIANS 5:18. *KJV.*

Some murmur, when their sky is clear
And wholly bright to view,
If one small speck of dark appear
In their great heaven of blue.
And some with thankful love are filled
If but one streak of light,
One ray of God's good mercy gild
The darkness of their night.
In palaces are hearts that ask,

In discontent and pride,
Why life is such a dreary task,
And all good things denied.
And hearts in poorest huts admire
How love has in their aid
(Love that not ever seems to tire)
Such rich provision made.

—Richard Chenevix Trench.
"Some Murmur, When Their Sky is Clear."
Sabbation; Honor Neale; and Other Poems.

The true felicity of life is to be free from perturbations; to understand our duties toward God and man; to enjoy the present without any anxious dependence upon the future. Not to amuse ourselves with either hopes or fears, but to rest satisfied with what we have, which is abundantly sufficient; for he that is so wants nothing. The great blessings of mankind are within us, and within our reach.

—Lucius Annaeus Seneca.
"Of A Happy Life." *Seneca's Morals by Way of Abstract.*

Thus humble let me live and die,
Nor long for Midas' golden touch;
If Heaven more generous gifts deny,
I shall not miss them much,
Too grateful for the blessing lent
Of simple tastes and mind content!

—Oliver Wendell Holmes.
"Contentment."

One single grateful thought raised to heaven is the most perfect prayer.

—Gotthold Ephraim Lessing.
Minna von Barnhelm.

However mean your life is, meet it and live it; do not shun it and call it hard names. It is not so bad as you are. It looks poorest when you are richest. The fault-finder will find faults even in paradise. Love your life, poor as it is. You may perhaps have some pleasant, thrilling, glorious hours, even in a poorhouse. The setting sun is reflected from the windows of the almshouse as brightly as from the rich man's abode; the snow melts before its door as early in the spring. I do not see but a quiet mind may live as contentedly there, and have as cheering thoughts, as in a palace.

—Henry David Thoreau.
Walden.

Thy mighty hand o'er all the land
Hath still been open to bestow
Those blessings which our wants demand
From heaven, whence all blessings flow.
Thou hast, with ever watchful eye,
Looked down on us with holy care,
And from thy storehouse in the sky
Hast scattered plenty everywhere.
Then lift we up our songs of praise
To thee, O Father, good and kind;

To thee we consecrate our days;
Be thine the temple of each mind.
With incense sweet our thanks ascend;
Before thy works our powers pall;
Though we should strive years without end,
We could not thank thee for them all.

—Paul Laurence Dunbar.
"A Thanksgiving Poem."

If we do our best; if we do not magnify trifling troubles; if we look resolutely, I do not say at the bright side of things, but at things as they really are; if we avail ourselves of the manifold blessings which surround us; we cannot but feel that life is indeed a glorious inheritance.

Few of us, however, realize the wonderful privilege of living, or the blessings we inherit; the glories and beauties of the Universe, which is our own if we choose to have it so; the extent to which we can make ourselves what we wish to be; or the power we possess of securing peace, of triumphing over pain and sorrow.

—Sir John Lubbock.
"The Duty of Happiness." *The Pleasures of Life.*

Thou that hast given so much to me,
Give one thing more, a grateful heart.

Not thankful when it pleaseth me,
As if thy blessings had spare days;
But such a heart, whose pulse may be thy praise.

—GEORGE HERBERT.
"Gratefulness."

So we should not overlook, but take account of everyday blessings, and rejoice that we live, and are well, and see the sun, and that no war or sedition plagues our country, but that the earth is open to cultivation, the sea secure to mariners, and that we can speak or be silent, lead a busy or an idle life, as we choose. We shall get more contentedness from the presence of all these blessings, if we fancy them as absent, and remember from time to time how people ill yearn for health, and people in war for peace, and strangers and unknown in a great city for reputation and friends, and how painful it is to be deprived of all these when one has once had them.

—PLUTARCH.
"On Contentedness of Mind."

So that you must be sure to inure yourself frequently to these principles and to impress them deeply; I will prize all I have, and nothing shall with me be less esteemed, because it is excellent. A daily joy shall be more my joy, because it is continual. A common joy is more my delight because it is common. For all mankind are my friends, and everything is enriched in serving them. A little grit in the eye destroyeth the sight of the very heavens, and a little malice or envy a world of joys. One wry principle in the mind is of infinite consequence. I will ever prize what I have, and so much the more because I have it. To prize a thing when it is gone breedeth torment and repining; to prize it while we have it joy and thanksgiving.

—THOMAS TRAHERNE.
Centuries of Meditations.

We ought to make the moments notes
Of happy, glad Thanksgiving;
The hours and days a silent phrase
Of music we are living.
And so the theme should swell and grow
As weeks and months pass o'er us,
And rise sublime at this good time,
A grand Thanksgiving chorus.

—ELLA WHEELER WILCOX.
"Thanksgiving." *Poems of Power.*

Thanks to you, sun and moon and star,
And you, blue level with no cloud, -
Thanks to you, splendors from afar,
For a high heart, a neck unbowed.

Thanks to you, wind, sent to and fro,
To you, light, pouring from the dawn;
Thanks for the breath and glory-flow
The steadfast soul can feed upon.

Thanks to you, pain and want and care,
And you, joys, cunning to deceive,
And you, balked phantoms of despair;
I battle on, and I believe.

—JOHN VANCE CHENEY.
"Thanks." *Poems.*

Chapter 21

ON COURAGE,
STRENGTH OF SPIRIT

Life, believe, is not a dream
So dark as sages say;
Oft a little morning rain
Foretells a pleasant day.
Sometimes there are clouds of gloom,
But these are transient all;
If the shower will make the roses bloom,
O why lament its fall?
Rapidly, merrily,
Life's sunny hours flit by,
Gratefully, cheerily
Enjoy them as they fly!
What though Death at times steps in,
And calls our Best away?
What though sorrow seems to win,
O'er hope, a heavy sway?
Yet Hope again elastic springs,
Unconquered, though she fell;
Still buoyant are her golden wings,
Still strong to bear us well.
Manfully, fearlessly,
The day of trial bear,

For gloriously, victoriously,
Can courage quell despair!

"Life."

We are troubled on every side, yet not distressed; we are perplexed, but not in despair;

Persecuted, but not forsaken; cast down, but not destroyed.

—2 Corinthians 4: 8-9. *KJV.*

Black as the Pit from pole to pole,
I thank whatever gods may be
For my unconquerable soul.
In the fell clutch of circumstance
I have not winced nor cried aloud.
Under the bludgeonings of chance
My head is bloody, but unbowed.
Beyond this place of wrath and tears
Looms but the Horror of the shade,
And yet the menace of the years
Finds, and shall find, me unafraid.
It matters not how strait the gate,
How charged with punishments the scroll.
I am the master of my fate:
I am the captain of my soul.

—William Ernest Henley.
"Invictus."

On Character, Conduct, Virtues   161

This is the time for his first lesson in courage, and by bearing slight ills without fear we gradually learn to bear greater.

—Jean-Jacques Rousseau.
Emile. Book II.

Thou must be like a promontory of the sea, against which though the waves beat continually, yet it both itself stands, and about it are those swelling waves stilled and quieted.

—Marcus Aurelius.
The Meditations of Marcus Aurelius.

O greater Maker of this Thy great sun,
Give me the strength this one day's race to run,
Fill me with light, fill me with sun-like strength,
Fill me with joy to rob the day its length.
Light from within, light that will outward shine,
Strength to make strong some weaker heart than mine,
Joy to make glad each soul that feels its touch;
Great Father of the sun, I ask this much.

—James Weldon Johnson.
"Prayer at Sunrise."

So let us also win the way to victory in all our struggles, - for the reward is not a garland or a palm or a trumpeter who calls for silence at the proclamation of our names, but rather virtue, steadfastness of soul, and a peace that is won for all time, if fortune has once been utterly vanquished in any combat.

—Lucius Annaeus Seneca.
"On the Healing Power of the Mind, Letter 78."
Moral letters to Lucilius.

When all their blooms the meadows flaunt
To deck the morning of the year,
Why tinge thy lustres jubilant
With forecast or with fear?
Teach me your mood, O patient stars!
Who climb each night the ancient sky,
Leaving on space no shade, no scars,
No trace of age, no fear to die.

—Ralph Waldo Emerson.
"Fragments on Nature and Life. Nature." *Poems.*

Grow old along with me!
The best is yet to be,
The last of life, for which the first was made:
Our times are in His hand
Who saith 'A whole I planned,
Youth shows but half; trust God: see all, nor be afraid!'

—Robert Browning.
"Rabbi Ben Ezra."

On Character, Conduct, Virtues   163

Conscience in the soul is the root of all true courage. If a man would be brave, let him obey his conscience.

—JAMES FREEMAN CLARKE.
"The Education of Courage." *Self-culture: Physical, Intellectual, Moral, and Spiritual: A Course of Lectures.*

The timid it concerns to ask their way,
And fear what foe in caves and swamps can stray,
To make no step until the event is known,
And ills to come as evils past bemoan.
Not so the wise; no coward watch he keeps
To spy what danger on his pathway creeps;
Go where he will, the wise man is at home,
His hearth the earth,—his hall the azure dome.

—RALPH WALDO EMERSON.
"Woodnotes I." *Poems.*

But thou, because thou hear'st
Men scoff at Heaven and Fate;
Because the gods thou fear'st
Fail to make blest thy state,
Tremblest, and wilt not dare to trust the joys there are.
I say, Fear not! life still
Leaves human effort scope.
But, since life teems with ill,
Nurse no extravagant hope.
Because thou must not dream, thou need'st not then despair.

—MATTHEW ARNOLD.
"Empedocles on Etna. Act I. Scene I."
Empedocles on Etna, and Other Poems.

But if man has, in all ages, had enough to encounter, there has, in most civilised ages, been an inward force vouchsafed him, whereby the pressure of things outward might be withstood. Obstruction abounded; but Faith also was not wanting. It is by Faith that man removes mountains: while he had Faith, his limbs might be wearied with toiling, his back galled with bearing; but the heart within him was peaceable and resolved. In the thickest gloom there burnt a lamp to guide him. If he struggled and suffered, he felt that it even should be so; knew for what he was suffering and struggling. Faith gave him an inward Willingness; a world of Strength wherewith to front a world of Difficulty.

—Thomas Carlyle.
"Characteristics."

There is a Power, whose care
Teaches thy way along that pathless coast,—
The desert and illimitable air
Lone wandering, but not lost.
All day thy wings have fanned,
At that far height, the cold thin atmosphere;
Yet stoop not, weary, to the welcome land,
Though the dark night is near.
And soon that toil shall end,
Soon shalt thou find a summer home, and rest,
And scream among thy fellows; reeds shall bend,
Soon, o'er thy sheltered nest.
Thou'rt gone, the abyss of heaven
Hath swallowed up thy form, yet, on my heart
Deeply hath sunk the lesson thou hast given,

And shall not soon depart.
He, who, from zone to zone,
Guides through the boundless sky thy certain flight,
In the long way that I must trace alone,
Will lead my steps aright.

—WILLIAM CULLEN BRYANT.
"To a Waterfowl."

Whoso calm, serene, sedate,
Sets his foot on haughty fate;
Firm and steadfast, come what will,
Keeps his mien unconquered still;
Him the rage of furious seas,
Tossing high wild menaces,
Nor the flames from smoky forges
That Vesuvius disgorges,
Nor the bolt that from the sky
Smites the tower, can terrify.
Why, then, shouldst thou feel affright
At the tyrant's weakling might?
Dread him not, nor fear no harm,
And thou shall his rage disarm;
But who to hope or fear gives way—
Lost his bosom's rightful sway—
He hath cast away his shield,
Like a coward fled the field;
He hath forged all unaware
Fetters his own neck must bear!

—BOETHIUS.
The Consolation of Philosophy of Boethius.

Chapter 22

ON NON-ATTACHMENT, DETACHMENT, LETTING GO

He who binds to himself a joy
Does the winged life destroy
He who kisses the joy as it flies
Lives in eternity's sunrise

—WILLIAM BLAKE.
"Eternity."

Sitting quietly, doing nothing, spring comes, and the grass grows by itself.

—BASHŌ MATSUO.

The Moving Finger writes: and, having writ,
Moves on: nor all thy Piety nor Wit
Shall lure it back to cancel half a Line,
Nor all thy Tears wash out a Word of it.

—OMAR KHAYYAM.
Rubaiyat of Omar Khayyam.

Only that man attains
Perfect surcease of work whose work was wrought
With mind unfettered, soul wholly subdued,
Desires for ever dead, results renounced.

—THE BHAGAVAD-GITA.

That is what is meant by working for duty. It makes all life comparatively easy. It makes it calm, strong, impartial, and undaunted; for the man does not cling to anything he does. When he has done it, he has no more concern with it. Let it go for success or failure as the world counts them, for he knows the Life within is ever going onwards to its goal. And it is the secret of peace in work, because those who work for success are always troubled, always anxious, always counting their forces, reckoning their chances and possibilities; but the man who cares nothing for success but only for duty, he works with the strength of divinity, and his aim is always sure.

—ANNIE BESANT.
The Meaning and Method of the Spiritual Life.

But he who, with strong body serving mind,
Gives up his mortal powers to worthy work,
Not seeking gain, Arjuna! such an one
Is honourable. Do thine allotted task!

—THE BHAGAVAD-GITA.

He must not only fly from sin and every occasion of sin, but he must shun all those things which drag him down from his higher aims; curiosity, self-complacency, love of praise, a desire to be of importance, all those trifles which distract the soul, and fix it upon earthly things. We need more watchfulness in this respect than it is our wont to give, for these external matters are the source of most men's predominant faults, and their great hindrance in the spiritual life.

The chief difficulty in attaining true detachment arises from our natural inclination to throw ourselves into the things of this world, and clinging to them, to seek a rest therein which they can never give.

—PERE JEAN NICOLAS GROU.
The Hidden Life of the Soul.

But, Arjun!
Abstaining from attachment to the work,
Abstaining from rewardment in the work,
While yet one doeth it full faithfully,
Saying, "Tis right to do!" that is "true " act
And abstinence! Who doeth duties so,
Unvexed if his work fail, if it succeed
Unflattered, in his own heart justified,
Quit of debates and doubts, his is "true" act:
For, being in the body, none may stand
Wholly aloof from act; yet, who abstains
From profit of his acts is abstinent.

—THE BHAGAVAD-GITA.

Chapter 23

ON JOY, HAPPINESS, CONTENTMENT

Oh happiness! our being's end and aim!
Good, pleasure, ease, content! whate'er thy name:
That something still which prompts th' eternal sigh,
For which we bear to live, or dare to die,
Which still so near us, yet beyond us lies,
O'er-look'd, seen double, by the fool, and wise.

—ALEXANDER POPE.
"Epistle IV". *An Essay on Man.*

There is not anything in this world, perhaps, that is more talked of, and less understood, than the business of a happy life. It is every man's wish and design; and yet not one of a thousand that knows wherein that happiness consists. We live, however, in a blind and eager pursuit of it; and the more haste we make in a wrong way, the further we are from our journey's end.

And the mischief is that the number of the multitude carries it against truth and justice.

So that we must leave the crowd if we would be happy: for the question of a happy life is not to be decided by vote: nay, so far from it, that plurality of voices is still an argument of the wrong; the common people find it easier to believe than to judge, and content themselves with what is usual, never examining whether it is good or not.

The true felicity of life is to be free from perturbations; to understand our duties toward God and man; to enjoy the present without any anxious dependence upon the future. Not to amuse ourselves with either hopes or fears, but to rest satisfied with what we have, which is abundantly sufficient; for he that is so wants nothing. The great blessings of mankind are within us, and within our reach; but we shut our eyes and, like people in the dark, we fall foul upon the very thing we search for without finding it. Tranquility is a certain equality of mind, which no condition of fortune can either exalt or depress. Nothing can make it less, for it is the state of human perfection.

—Lucius Annaeus Seneca.
"Of A Happy Life." *Seneca's Morals by Way of Abstract.*

Herein doth consist happiness of life, for a man to know thoroughly the true nature of everything; what is the matter, and what is the form of it: with all his heart and soul, ever to do that which is just, and to speak the truth. What then remaineth but to enjoy thy life in a course and coherence of good actions, one upon another immediately succeeding, and never interrupted, though for never so little a while?

—Marcus Aurelius.
The Meditations of Marcus Aurelius.

The disturbers of our happiness, in this world, are our desires, our griefs, and our fears; and to all these, the consideration of mortality is a certain and adequate remedy. Think, says Epictetus, frequently on poverty, banishment, and death, and thou wilt then never indulge violent desires, or give up thy heart to mean sentiments.

—Samuel Johnson.
"No. 17." *The Rambler.*

The pleasures of youth may excel in keenness and in zest, but they have at the best a tinge of anxiety and unrest; they cannot have the fulness and depth which may accompany the consolations of age, and are amongst the richest rewards of an unselfish life. For as with the close of the day, so with that of life; there may be clouds, and yet if the horizon is clear, the evening may be beautiful.

—Sir John Lubbock.
"The Destiny of Man." *The Pleasures of Life.*

These are the gifts I ask
Of thee, Spirit serene:
Strength for the daily task,
Courage to face the road,
Good cheer to help me bear the traveller's load,
And, for the hours of rest that come between,
An inward joy in all things heard and seen.
These are the sins I fain
Would have thee take away:

Malice, and cold disdain,
Hot anger, sullen hate,
Scorn of the lowly, envy of the great,
And discontent that casts a shadow gray
On all the brightness of the common day.

These are the things I prize
And hold of dearest worth:
Light of the sapphire skies,
Peace of the silent hills,
Shelter of forests, comfort of the grass,
Music of birds, murmur of little rills,
Shadow of clouds that swiftly pass,
And, after showers,
The smell of flowers
And of the good brown earth,—
And best of all, along the way, friendship and mirth.

—HENRY VAN DYKE.
"God of the Open Air."

Do not think it then either your business, or an easy matter either, to set all these things to rights. But if you take people as they are, as the surgeon uses his bandages and instruments for drawing teeth, and with cheerfulness and serenity welcome all that happens, as you would look upon barking dogs as only following their nature, you will be happier in the disposition you will then have than you will be distressed at other people's disagreeableness and shortcomings.

It also makes for contentedness, when things happen against our wish, not to overlook our many advantages and comforts, but by looking at both good and bad to feel that the good preponderate.

—PLUTARCH.
"On Contentedness of Mind."

Work indeed, and hard work, if only it is in moderation, is in itself a rich source of happiness. We all know how quickly time passes when we are well employed, while the moments hang heavily on the hands of the idle. Occupation drives away care and all the small troubles of life. The busy man has no time to brood or to fret.

—SIR JOHN LUBBOCK.
"Labor and Rest." *The Pleasures of Life.*

It is good to tame the mind, which is difficult to hold in and flighty, rushing wherever it listeth; a tamed mind brings happiness.

Let the wise man guard his thoughts, for they are difficult to perceive, very artful, and they rush wherever they list: thoughts well guarded bring happiness.

—*THE DHAMMAPADA.*

The amiableness of virtue consisteth in this, that by it all happiness is either attained or enjoyed. Contentment and rest ariseth from a full perception of infinite treasures. So that whosoever will profit in the mystery of Felicity, must see the objects of his happiness, and the manner how they are to be enjoyed, and discern also the powers of his soul by which he is to enjoy them, and perhaps the rules that shall guide him in the way of enjoyment. All which you have here, God, the world, your self, all things in Time and Eternity being the objects of your Felicity, God the Giver, and you the receiver.

—THOMAS TRAHERNE.
Centuries of Meditations.

I weigh not fortune's frown or smile;
I joy not much in earthly joys;
I seek not state, I reck not style;
I am not fond of fancy's toys:
I rest so pleased with what I have,
I wish no more, no more I crave.

I feign not friendship where I hate;
I fawn not on the great (in show);
I prize, I praise a mean estate,—
Neither too lofty nor too low:
This, this is all my choice, my cheer,—
A mind content, a conscience clear.

—JOSHUA SYLVESTER.
"A Contented Mind."

That maxim also which your friend used is of very great and Divine concernment: "I will first spend a great deal of time in seeking Happiness, and then a great deal more in enjoying it." For if Happiness be worthy to be sought, it is worthy to be enjoyed. As no folly in the world is more vile than that pretended by alchemists, of having the Philosopher's Stone and being contented without using it: so is no deceit more odious, than that of spending many days in studying, and none in enjoying, happiness.

—Thomas Traherne. *Centuries of Meditations.*

…the fountain of content must spring up in the mind; and he, who has so little knowledge of human nature, as to seek happiness by changing any thing, but his own dispositions, will waste his life in fruitless efforts, and multiply the griefs which he purposes to remove.

—Samuel Johnson. "No. 6." *The Rambler.*

To be wise we must first learn to be happy, that we may attach ever smaller importance to what happiness may be in itself. We should be as happy as possible, and our happiness should last as long as is possible; for those who can finally issue forth from self by the portal of happiness, know infinitely wider freedom than those who pass through the gate of sadness. The joy of the sage illumines his heart and his soul alike, whereas sadness most often throws light on the heart alone.

—Maurice Maeterlinck. *Wisdom and Destiny.*

'Why, then, ye children of mortality, seek ye from without that happiness whose seat is only within us? Error and ignorance bewilder you. I will show thee, in brief, the hinge on which perfect happiness turns. Is there anything more precious to thee than thyself? Nothing, thou wilt say. If, then, thou art master of thyself, thou wilt possess that which thou wilt never be willing to lose, and which Fortune cannot take from thee. And that thou mayst see that happiness cannot possibly consist in these things which are the sport of chance, reflect that, if happiness is the highest good of a creature living in accordance with reason, and if a thing which can in any wise be reft away is not the highest good, since that which cannot be taken away is better than it, it is plain that Fortune cannot aspire to bestow happiness by reason of its instability.

—BOETHIUS.
"Book II." *The Consolation of Philosophy of Boethius.*

True contentment is neither merry nor noisy; we are jealous of so sweet a sentiment, when we enjoy it we think about it, we delight in it for fear it should escape us. A really happy man says little and laughs little; he hugs his happiness, so to speak, to his heart.

—JEAN-JACQUES ROUSSEAU.
Emile, or Education. Book IV.

My heart is like a little bird
That sits and sings for very gladness.
Sorrow is some forgotten word,
And so, except in rhyme, is sadness.
The world is very fair to me –
Such azure skies, such golden weather,
I'm like a long caged bird set free,
My heart is lighter than a feather.
I rise rejoicing in my life;
I live with love of God and neighbour;
My days flow on unmarred by strife,
And sweetened by my pleasant labour.
O youth! O spring! O happy days,
Ye are so passing sweet, and tender,
And while the fleeting season stays,
I revel care-free, in its splendour.

—ELLA WHEELER WILCOX.
"Joy."

Active in indolence, abroad we roam
In quest of happiness which dwells at home:
With vain pursuits fatigu'd, at length you'll find,
No place excludes it from an equal mind.

—HORACE.
"Ep. xi. lib. i." *The Rambler.*

I asked myself: What is this that, ever since earliest years, thou hast been fretting and fuming, and lamenting and self-tormenting, on account of? Say it in a word: is it not because thou art not HAPPY? Because the THOU (sweet gentleman) is not sufficiently honored, nourished, soft-bedded, and lovingly cared for? Foolish soul! What Act of Legislature was there that *thou* shouldst be Happy? A little while ago thou hadst no right to *be* at all. What if thou wert born and predestined not to be Happy, but to be Unhappy! Art thou nothing other than a Vulture, because carrion enough is not given thee? Close thy *Byron*; open thy *Goethe*.

—THOMAS CARLYLE.
Sartor Resartus.

Happy the man, of mortals happiest he,
Whose quiet mind from vain desires is free;
Whom neither hopes deceive, nor fears torment,
But lives at peace, within himself content,
In thought, or act, accountable to none,
But to himself, and to the gods alone:
O sweetness of content! Seraphic joy!
Which nothing wants, and nothing can destroy.

—GEORGE GRANVILLE, LORD LANSDOWNE.
"Epistle to Mrs. Elizabeth Higgons, 1690."
Poems of George Granville, Lord Lansdowne.

Chapter 24

On Giving,
Charity, Generosity

The Master desires no possessions.
Since the things she does are for the people,
she has more than she needs.
The more she gives to others,
the more she has for herself.

—Lao Tzu.
The Tao Te Ching.

See the rivers flowing
Downwards to the sea,
Pouring all their treasures
Bountiful and free—
Yet to help their giving
Hidden springs arise;
Or, if need be, showers
Feed them from the skies!

Watch the princely flowers
Their rich fragrance spread,
Load the air with perfumes,
From their beauty shed—

Yet their lavish spending
Leaves them not in dearth,
With fresh life replenished
By their mother earth!

Give thy heart's best treasures—
From fair Nature learn;
Give thy love—and ask not,
Wait not a return!
And the more thou spendest
From thy little store,
With a double bounty,
God will give thee more.

—ADELAIDE ANNE PROCTER. "Give."

What I have, I will not either sordidly spare, or prodigally squander away, and I will reckon upon benefits well-placed as the fairest part of my possession: not valuing them by number or weight, but by profit and esteem of the receiver; accounting myself never the poorer for that which I give to a worthy person.

—LUCIUS ANNAEUS SENECA.
"Of a Happy Life."

Every man according as he purposeth in his heart, so let him give; not grudgingly, or of necessity: for God loveth a cheerful giver.

—2 CORINTHIANS 9:7. *KJV.*

There is a great subtlety in giving what costs little yet is much desired, so that it is esteemed the more.

—Baltasar Gracian.
The Art of Worldly Wisdom.

I have shewed you all things, how that so labouring ye ought to support the weak, and to remember the words of the Lord Jesus, how he said, It is more blessed to give than to receive.

—Acts 20:35. *KJV.*

Far other aims his heart had learn'd to prize—
More skill'd to raise the wretched than to rise.
His house was known to all the vagrant train;
He chid their wanderings, but reliev'd their pain;
The long-remember'd beggar was his guest,
Whose beard descending swept his aged breast;
The ruin'd spendthrift, now no longer proud,
Claim'd kindred there, and had his claim allow'd;
The broken soldier, kindly bade to stay,
Sat by his fire, and talk'd the night away—
Wept o'er his wounds, or, tales of sorrow done,
Shoulder'd his crutch, and show'd how fields were won.
Pleas'd with his guests, the good man learn'd to glow,
And quite forgot their vices in their woe;
Careless their merits or their faults to scan,
His pity gave ere charity began.

—Oliver Goldsmith. "The Deserted Village."

There are those who give little of the much which they have - and they give it for recognition and their hidden desire makes their gifts unwholesome. And there are those who have little and give it all. These are the believers in life and the bounty of life, and their coffer is never empty.

There are those who give with joy, and that joy is their reward. And there are those who give with pain, and that pain is their baptism.

And there are those who give and know not pain in giving, nor do they seek joy, nor give with mindfulness of virtue; They give as in yonder valley the myrtle breathes its fragrance into space. Though the hands of such as these God speaks, and from behind their eyes He smiles upon the earth.

—KAHLIL GIBRAN.
The Prophet.

If there be among you a poor man of one of thy brethren within any of thy gates in thy land which the Lord thy God giveth thee, thou shalt not harden thine heart, nor shut thine hand from thy poor brother:

But thou shalt open thine hand wide unto him, and shalt surely lend him sufficient for his need, in that which he wanteth.

—DEUTERONOMY 15: 7-8. *KJV.*

The gift lovingly given, when one shall say
"Now must I gladly give!" when he who takes
Can render nothing back; made in due place,
Due time, and to a meet recipient,
Is gift of Sattwan, fair and profitable.
The gift selfishly given, where to receive
Is hoped again, or when some end is sought,
Or where the gift is proffered with a grudge,
This is of Rajas, stained with impulse, ill.
The gift churlishly flung, at evil time,
In wrongful place, to base recipient,
Made in disdain or harsh unkindliness,
Is gift of Tamas, dark; it doth not bless!

—THE BHAGAVAD-GITA.

The Holy Supper is kept, indeed,
In whatso we share with another's need,—
Not that which we give, but what we share,—
For the gift without the giver is bare;
Who bestows himself with his alms feeds three,—
Himself, his hungering neighbor, and me.

—JAMES RUSSELL LOWELL.
"The Vision of Sir Launfal."
The Vision of Sir Launfal and Other Poems.

The tone in which we speak to the world, the world speaks to us. Give your best and you will get the best in return. Give in heaping measure and in heaping measure it shall be returned. We all get our due sooner or later, in one form or another. "Be not weary in well doing;" the reward will surely come, if not in worldly goods, then in inward satisfaction, grace of spirit, peace of mind.

—JOHN BURROUGHS.
"An Outlook Upon Life." *Leaf and Tendril.*

In Faith and Hope the world will disagree,
But all mankind's concern is Charity:
All must be false that thwart this one great end,
And all of God that bless mankind or mend.

—ALEXANDER POPE.
"Epistle III." *Essay on Man.*

Chapter 25

ON DUTY, SERVICE, RIGHT ACTION

The sweetest lives are those to duty wed,
Whose deeds, both great and small,
Are close knit strands of an unbroken thread,
Whose love ennobles all.
The world may sound no trumpet, ring no bells;
The book of life, the slurring record tells.
Thy love shall chant its own beatitudes,
After its own life-working. A child's kiss
Set on thy singing lips shall make thee glad;
A poor man served by thee shall make thee rich;
A sick man helped by thee shall make thee strong;
Thou shalt be served thyself by every sense
Of service thou renderest.

—ELIZABETH BARRETT BROWNING.
"Reward of Service."

That is what is meant by working for duty. It makes all life comparatively easy. It makes it calm, strong, impartial, and undaunted; for the man does not cling to anything he does. When he has done it, he has no more concern with it. Let it go for success or failure as the world counts them, for he knows the Life within is ever going onwards to its goal. And it is the secret of peace in work, because those who work for success are always troubled, always anxious, always counting their forces, reckoning their chances and possibilities; but the man who cares nothing for success but only for duty, he works with the strength of divinity, and his aim is always sure.

—ANNIE BESANT.
The Meaning and Method of Spiritual Life.

Yet how do you know what you may lose by neglecting this duty, which you think so trifling, or the blessing which its faithful performance may bring?

Be sure that if you do your very best in that which is laid upon you daily, you will not be left without sufficient help when some weightier occasion arises.

—PERE JEAN NICOLAS GROU.
The Hidden Life of the Soul.

But he who, with strong body serving mind,
Gives up his mortal powers to worthy work,
Not seeking gain, Arjuna! such an one
Is honourable. Do thine allotted task!
Work is more excellent than idleness;
The body's life proceeds not, lacking work.
There is a task of holiness to do,

Unlike world-binding toil, which bindeth not
The faithful soul; such earthly duty do
Free from desire, and thou shalt well perform
Thy heavenly purpose.

—The Bhagavad-Gita.

On which ground, too, let him who gropes painfully in darkness or uncertain light, and prays vehemently that the dawn may ripen into day, lay this other precept well to heart, which to me was of invaluable service: '*Do the Duty which lies nearest thee,*' which thou knowest to be a Duty! Thy second Duty will already have become clearer.

—Thomas Carlyle.
Sartor Resartus.

Therefore, thy task prescribed
With spirit unattached gladly perform,
Since in performance of plain duty man
Mounts to his highest bliss.

—The Bhagavad-Gita.

Not to ease and aimless quiet
Doth that inward answer tend,
But to works of love and duty
As our being's end;
Not to idle dreams and trances,
Length of face, and solemn tone,
But to Faith, in daily striving
And performance shown.

—JOHN GREENLEAF WHITTIER.
"To——, with a Copy of Woolman's Journal."

So every duty, even the least duty, involves the whole principle of obedience. And little duties make the will dutiful, that is, supple and prompt to obey. Little obediences lead into great.

The daily round of duty is full of probation and of discipline; it trains the will, heart, and conscience. To be holy we need not to be prophets or apostles. The commonest life may be full of perfection. The duties of home are a discipline for the ministries of heaven.

—HENRY EDWARD MANNING.
Sermons, Volume the Fourth.

Let us do our duty in our shop or our kitchen, the market, the street, the office, the school, the home, just as faithfully as if we stood in the front rank of some great battle, and we knew that victory for mankind depended upon our bravery, strength, and skill. When we do that the humblest of us will be serving in that great army which achieves the welfare of the world.

—THEODORE PARKER.
"Traits and Illustrations of Human Character and Conduct."
The Collected Works of Theodore Parker: Volume XIV.
Lessons from the World of Matter and the World of Man.

Now the relative duties of life are universal. Every man has his own. There is nothing peculiar but that which belongs to each man's peculiar station, and that station explains the peculiarity of his acts and ways. Whatever we are, high or lowly, learned or unlearned, married or single, in a full house or alone, charged with many affairs or dwelling in quietness, we have our daily round of work, our duties of affection, obedience, love, mercy, industry, and the like; and that which makes one man to differ from another is not so much what things he does, as his manner of doing them.

—HENRY EDWARD MANNING.
Sermons. Volume the Second.

Duty is a power which rises with us in the morning, and goes to rest with us at night. It is coextensive with the action of our intelligence. It is the shadow which cleaves to us, go where we will, and which only leaves us when we leave the light of life.

—WILLIAM EWART GLADSTONE.
The Vatican Decrees in Their Bearing on Civil Allegiance.

Yet on the nimble air benign
Speed nimbler messages,
That waft the breath of grace divine
To hearts in sloth and ease.
So nigh is grandeur to our dust,
So near is God to man.
When Duty whispers low, Thou must,
The youth replies, I can.

—RALPH WALDO EMERSON.
"Voluntaries." *May-day, and Other Pieces.*

Chapter 26

ON VIRTUE

Virtue, the strength and beauty of the soul,
Is the best gift of heaven: a happiness
That even above the smiles and frowns of fate
Exalts great Nature's favourites: a wealth
That ne'er incumbers, nor to baser hands
Can be transferr'd: it is the only good
Man justly boasts of, or can call his own.

—JOHN ARMSTRONG.
"Book IV." *The Art of Preserving Health: A Poem.*

No one who is a lover of money, a lover of pleasure, or a lover of glory, is likewise a lover of mankind; but only he who is a lover of virtue.

—EPICTETUS.
"Fragments." *All the Works of Epictetus,*
which are Now Extant.

I think vital religion has always suffered when orthodoxy is more regarded than virtue. The scriptures assure me that at the last day we shall not be examined on what we thought but what we did.

—BENJAMIN FRANKLIN.
"To Josiah Franklin." (Letter to his father, 1738.)

There is in Virtue a dignity of her own which she forthwith passes over to those to whom she is united.

—BOETHIUS.
"Book III." *The Consolation of Philosophy of Boethius.*

O Thou bright jewel in my aim I strive
To comprehend thee. Thine own words declare
Wisdom is higher than a fool can reach.
I cease to wonder, and no more attempt
Thine height t' explore, or fathom thy profound.
But, O my soul, sink not into despair,
Virtue is near thee, and with gentle hand
Would now embrace thee, hovers o'er thine head.
Fain would the heav'n-born soul with her converse,
Then seek, then court her for her promis'd bliss.
Auspicious queen, thine heav'nly pinions spread,
And lead celestial Chastity along;
Lo! now her sacred retinue descends,
Array'd in glory from the orbs above.
Attend me, Virtue, thro' my youthful years!
O leave me not to the false joys of time!

But guide my steps to endless life and bliss.
Greatness, or Goodness, say what I shall call thee,
To give me an higher appellation still,
Teach me a better strain, a nobler lay,
O thou, enthron'd with Cherubs in the realms of day.

—PHILLIS WHEATLEY.
"On Virtue."

Virtue is the sun of the microcosm, and has for hemisphere a good conscience. She is so beautiful that she finds favour with both God and man. Nothing is lovable but virtue, nothing detestable but vice. Virtue alone is serious, all else is but jest. A man's capacity and greatness are to be measured by his virtue and not by his fortune. She alone is all-sufficient. She makes men lovable in life, memorable after death.

—BALTASAR GRACIAN.
The Art of Wordly Wisdom.

It is virtue that uplifts man and places him superior to what mortals hold dear; virtue neither craves overmuch nor fears to excess that which is called good or that which is called bad.

—LUCIUS ANNAEUS SENECA.
"Epistle LXXXVII. Some Arguments
in Favor of the Simple Life."

"This above all: to thine own self be true,
And it must follow, as the night the day,
Thou canst not then be false to any man."

—WILLIAM SHAKESPEARE.
Hamlet.

Sandal–wood or Tagara, a lotus–flower, or a Vassiki, among these sorts of perfumes, the perfume of virtue is unsurpassed.

Mean is the scent that comes from Tagara and sandal–wood; –– the perfume of those who possess virtue rises up to the gods as the highest.

Of the people who possess these virtues, who live without thoughtlessness, and who are emancipated through true knowledge, Mara, the tempter, never finds the way.

—THE DHAMMAPADA.

Moral precepts, which to a superficial view appear arbitrary, and seem made to spoil our zest for life, have really but one object-to preserve us from the evil of having lived in vain.

—CHARLES WAGNER.
The Simple Life.

What, what is virtue, but repose of mind,
A pure ethereal calm, that knows no storm;
Above the reach of wild ambition's wind,
Above those passions that this world deform.

—JAMES THOMSON.
"Canto I." *Castle of Indolence. An Allegorical Poem.*

But the social passions never afford such transporting pleasures, or make so glorious an appearance in the eyes of both God and man, as when, shaking off every earthly mixture, they associate themselves with the sentiments of virtue, and prompt us to laudable and worthy actions. As harmonious colours mutually give and receive a lustre by their friendly union; so do these ennobling sentiments of the human mind.

Happy the man, whom indulgent fortune allows to pay to virtue what he owes to nature, and to make a generous gift of what must otherwise be ravished from him by cruel necessity.

The man of morals is satisfied with the portion marked out to him by the Supreme Disposer of all things. Gratefully he accepts of that farther reward prepared for him; but if, disappointed, he thinks not virtue an empty name; but justly esteeming it its own reward, he gratefully acknowledges the bounty of his Creator, who by calling him into existence, has thereby afforded him an opportunity of once acquiring so invaluable a possession.

—DAVID HUME.
"Essay 16: The Stoic." *Essays Moral,*
Political, and Literary, Volume 1.

Chapter 27

ON NON-ACTION,
NON-RESISTANCE

One who seeks knowledge learns something new every day.
One who seeks the Tao unlearns something new every day.
Less and less remains until you arrive at non-action.
When you arrive at non-action,
nothing will be left undone.
Mastery of the world is achieved
by letting things take their natural course.
You can not master the world by changing the natural way.

—LAO TZU.
Tao Te Ching.

A little consideration of what takes place around us every day would show us that a higher law than that of our will regulates events; that our painful labors are unnecessary and fruitless; that only in our easy, simple, spontaneous action are we strong, and by contenting ourselves with obedience we become divine.

—RALPH WALDO EMERSON.
"Spiritual Laws." *Essays, First Series.*

Act by not acting;
do by not doing.
Enjoy the plain and simple.
Find that greatness in the small.
Take care of difficult problems
while they are still easy;
Do easy things before they become too hard.
Difficult problems are best solved while they are easy.
Great projects are best started while they are small.
The Master never takes on more than she can handle,
which means that she leaves nothing undone.

—LAO TZU.
Tao Te Ching.

Give what thou wilt, and take away what thou wilt, saith
he that is well taught and truly modest, to Him that gives,
and takes away. And it is not out of a stout and peremptory
resolution, that he saith it, but in mere love, and humble
submission.

—MARCUS AURELIUS.
The Meditations of Marcus Aurelius.

Water is the softest and most yielding substance.
Yet nothing is better than water,
for overcoming the hard and rigid,
because nothing can compete with it.
Everyone knows that the soft and yielding
overcomes the rigid and hard,
but few can put this knowledge into practice.

—Lao Tzu.
Tao Te Ching.

Sitting quietly, doing nothing, spring comes, and the grass grows by itself.

—Bashō Matsuo.

The chief pang of most trials is not so much the actual suffering itself, as our own spirit of resistance to it. But a soul that accepts its own nothingness is free from this resistance, and nothing can disturb its peace – the habit of renunciation strengthens continually, and we are astonished to find ourselves bearing that which once seemed intolerable, calmly and patiently.

—Pere Jean Nicolas Grou.
The Hidden Life of the Soul.

Peace does not dwell in outward things, but within the soul. We may preserve it in the midst of the bitterest pain, if our will remains firm and submissive. Peace in this life springs from acquiescence even in disagreeable things, not in an exemption from bearing them.

—Francois de Salignac de La Mothe Fénelon.
Selections from Fénelon.

Go on in all simplicity; do not be so anxious to win a quiet mind, and it will be all the quieter. Do not examine so closely into the progress of your soul. Do not crave so much to be perfect, but let your spiritual life be formed by your duties, and by the actions which are called forth by circumstances. Do not take overmuch thought for to-morrow.

—St. Francis de Sales.
A Selection from the Spiritual Letters of s. Francis de Sales.

Chapter 28

On Talking, Speech, Silence

Command your temper, guard your tongue,
Lest they have sway undue;
For deeds, not words, the bell be rung,
Which fame may ring for you!

—Frances S. Osgood.
"Golden Rules in Rhymes." *Poems.*

One should speak well and act honourably: the one is an excellence of the head, the other of the heart, and both arise from nobility of soul. Words are the shadows of deeds; the former are feminine, the latter masculine. It is more important to be renowned than to convey renown. Speech is easy, action hard. Actions are the stuff of life, words its frippery. Eminent deeds endure, striking words pass away. Actions are the fruit of thought; if this is wise, they are effective.

—Baltasar Gracian.
The Art of Worldly Wisdom.

If aught good thou canst not say
Of thy brother, foe, or friend,
Take thou, then, the silent way,
Lest in word thou shouldst offend.

—ANONYMOUS.
The Speaker's Garland. Volume 9.

Go placidly amid the noise and haste and remember what peace there may be in silence.

—MAX EHRMANN.
"Desiderata."

Be not rash with thy mouth, and let not thine heart be hasty to utter any thing before God: for God is in heaven, and thou upon earth: therefore let thy words be few.

—ECCLESIASTES 5:2. *KJV.*

......and a fool's voice is known by multitude of words.

—ECCLESIASTES 5:3. *KJV.*

And there are those who talk, and without knowledge or forethought reveal a truth which they themselves do not understand. And there are those who have the truth within them, but they tell it not in words. In the bosom of such as these the spirit dwells in rhythmic silence.

—KAHLIL GIBRAN.
The Prophet.

Those who know do not talk.
Those who talk do not know.
Stop talking,
meditate in silence,
blunt your sharpness,
release your worries,
harmonize your inner light,
and become one with the dust.
Doing this is the called the dark and mysterious identity.

—LAO TZU.
Tao Te Ching.

A soft answer turneth away wrath: but grievous words stir up anger.

The tongue of the wise useth knowledge aright: but the mouth of fools poureth out foolishness.

—PROVERBS 15:1-2. *KJV.*

Silence humbles our spirit, and gradually detaches it from the world; it constitutes in the heart a sort of solitude like that you so much long after, and will supply all your wants in the many perplexities that surround you. If we never unnecessarily open our mouths, we may enjoy many moments of communion even when unavoidably detained in society.

—François de Salignac de la Mothe Fénelon.
Spiritual Progress.

Give every man thy ear but few thy voice.

—William Shakespeare. *Hamlet.*

Avoid the company of drunkards and busybodies, and all such as are apt to talk much to little purpose; for no man can be provident of his time that is not prudent in the choice of his company; and if one of the speakers be vain, tedious, and trifling, he that hears, and he that answers in the discourse, are equal losers of their time.

—Jeremy Taylor. *The Rules and Exercises of Holy Living.*

Words causing no man woe, words ever true,
Gentle and pleasing words, and those ye say
In murmured reading of a Sacred Writ,—
These make the true religiousness of Speech.

—*The Bhagavad-Gita.*

Speech is the chief revelation of the mind, the first visible form that it takes. As the thought, so the speech. To better one's life in the way of simplicity, one must set a watch on his lips and his pen. Let the word be as genuine as the thought, as artless, as valid: think justly, speak frankly.

—CHARLES WAGNER.
The Simple Life.

Among the sources of those innumerable calamities which from age to age have overwhelmed mankind, may be reckoned as one of the principal the abuse of words.

—BISHOP GEORGE HORNE.
Prose Quotations from Socrates to Macaulay.

Companion none is like unto the mind alone,
For many have been harmed by speech, - through thinking,
few or none;
Fear oftentimes restraineth words, but makes not thought
to cease;
And he speaks best that hath the skill when for to hold
his peace.

—THOMAS, LORD VAUX.
"Of a Contented Spirit."

But there is another kind of silence to be cultivated besides that of the tongue as regards others. I mean silence as regards one's self –– restraining the imagination, not permitting it to dwell overmuch on what we have heard or said, not indulging in the phantasmagoria of picture-thoughts, whether of the past or future.

—PERE JEAN NICOLAS GROU.
The Hidden Life of the Soul.

In silence was the Universe conceived,
In silence doth the heart of man seek out
That other heart to rest on; Nature's soul
Yearns ceaselessly to give its speechless calm
Unto her restless children as they roam
Far from that central place which is their home.

Wouldst know thy Mother Nature face to face?
Wouldst hear her silent heartbeats? Close thine ears
And still thy senses; wouldst thou feel her arms
Enfold thy being? Thou must give thyself
In uttermost abandon to her will
That she may teach thee the one truth – be still!

Be still – and from the Silences shall arise
A mem'ry of forgotten mysteries.
A healing peace descending on thy soul
Shall bear it up to regions beyond words
Where thou shalt learn the secrets of the earth.
Of wind and flame and how the stars have birth.

Then shalt thou know thy heritage of joy;

Born on the pinions of the Bird of Life,
Tuned to the rhythm of revolving spheres,
Feeling with all that breathes, with all that strives
With union with its prototype above,
The silent comforter whose name is – Love.

—M. Frances Poile.
"Silence."

Chapter 29

On Inner Peace, Equanimity, Tranquility

Come, peace of mind, delightful guest!
Return and make thy downy nest
Once more in this sad heart:
Nor riches I, nor pow'r pursue,
Nor hold forbidden joys in view,
We therefore need not part.

Where wilt thou dwell if not with me,
From av'rice and ambition free,
And pleasure's fatal wiles?
For whom, alas! dost thou prepare
The sweets that I was wont to share,
The banquet of thy smiles?

—WILLIAM COWPER.
"Ode to Peace."

Calmness of mind is one of the beautiful jewels of wisdom. It is the result of long and patient effort in self-control. Its presence is an indication of ripened experience, and of a more than ordinary knowledge of the laws and operations of thought.

—JAMES ALLEN.
As A Man Thinketh.

Hope gives rise to extravagant promises which experience does not fulfill. Such idle imaginations merely serve as a well-spring of annoyance when disillusion comes with the true reality. The wise man anticipates such errors: he may always hope for the best, but he always expects the worst, so as to receive what comes with equanimity.

—BALTASAR GRACIAN.
The Art of Worldly Wisdom.

Krishna.
He who with equanimity surveys
Lustre of goodness, strife of passion, sloth
Of ignorance, not angry if they are,
Not wishful when they are not: he who sits
A sojourner and stranger in their midst
Unruffled, standing off, saying—serene—
When troubles break, "These be the Qualities!"
He unto whom—self-centred—grief and joy
Sound as one word; to whose deep-seeing eyes
The clod, the marble, and the gold are one;

Whose equal heart holds the same gentleness
For lovely and unlovely things, firm-set,
Well-pleased in praise and dispraise; satisfied
With honour or dishonour; unto friends
And unto foes alike in tolerance;
Detached from undertakings,—he is named
Surmounter of the Qualities!

—THE BHAGAVAD-GITA.

We refuse to be unduly depressed in the gloom, as we refused to be unduly elated in the light; we balance one experience against the other, removing the thorn of present pain by the memory of past joy and the foretaste of joy in the future; we learn in happiness to remember sorrow and in sorrow to remember happiness, till neither the one nor the other can shake the steady foothold of the soul. Thus we begin to rise above the lower stages of consciousness in which we are flung from one extreme to the other, and to gain the equilibrium which is called yoga. Thus the existence of the law becomes to us not a theory but a conviction, and we gradually learn something of the peace of the Self.

—ANNIE BESANT.
"Some Difficulties of the Inner Life."

Tranquility is a certain equality of mind, which no condition of fortune can either exalt or depress. Nothing can make it less, for it is the state of human perfection.

—Lucius Annaeus Seneca.
"Of a Happy Life."

Go placidly amid the noise and haste and remember what peace there may be in silence.

—Max Ehrmann.
"Desiderata."

That exquisite poise of character, which we call serenity is the last lesson of culture, the fruitage of the soul. It is precious as wisdom, more to be desired than gold—yea, than even fine gold. How insignificant mere money seeking looks in comparison with a serene life—a life that dwells in the ocean of Truth, beneath the waves, beyond the reach of tempests, in the Eternal Calm!

—James Allen.
As A Man Thinketh.

"I saw a delicate flower had grown up two feet high, between the horses' path and the wheel track. Which Dakin's and Maynard's wagons had passed over many a time. An inch more to right or left had sealed its fate, or an inch higher; and yet it lived to flourish as much as it had a thousand acres of untrodden space around it, and never knew the danger it incurred. It didn't borrow trouble, nor invite an evil fate by apprehending it."

—HENRY DAVID THOREAU.
The Writings of Henry David Thoreau: Journal, Volume 8.

It has been said that "in patience ye shall win your souls," and what is this patience but an equanimity which enables you to rise superior to the trials of life? Sowing as you shall do beside all waters, I can but wish that you may reap the promised blessing of quietness and of assurance forever, until

Within this life,

Though lifted o'er its strife,

you may, in the growing winters, glean a little of that wisdom which is pure, peaceable, gentle, full of mercy and good fruits, without partiality and without hypocrisy.

—WILLIAM OSLER.
Aequanimitas.

So true is it that nothing is wretched, but thinking makes it so, and conversely every lot is happy if borne with equanimity.

—BOETHIUS.
The Consolation of Philosophy.

Require not Things to happen as you wish; but wish them
to happen as they do happen; and you will go on well.

—EPICTETUS.
"VIII." *The Enchiridion.*

Thou precious treasure of the peaceful mind,
Thou jewel of inestimable price,
Thou bravest soul's terrestrial paradise,
Dearest contentment, thou best happiness
That man on earth can know,
Thou greatest gift Heav'n can on man bestow,
And greater than man's language can express;
(Where highest epithets would fall so low,
As only in our dearth of words to show
A part of thy perfection; a poor part
Of what to us, what in thyself thou art)
What sin has banish'd thee the world,
And in thy stead despairing sorrow hurl'd
Into the breasts of humankind;
Ah whither art thou fled! Who can this treasure find!

—CHARLES COTTON.
"Contentment. Pindaric Ode."

Chapter 30

ON SIMPLICITY, SMALL THINGS, THE ESSENTIALS

Our portion is not large, indeed!
But then how little do we need!
For nature's calls are few:
In this the art of living lies,
To want no more than may suffice,
And make that little do.

We'll therefore relish, with content,
Whate'er kind Providence has sent,
Nor aim beyond our pow'r;
For if our stock be very small,
'Tis prudence to enjoy it all
Nor lose the present hour.

—NATHANIEL COTTON.
"The Fire-Side."

Simplicity is a state of mind. It dwells in the main intention of our lives. A man is simple when his chief care is the wish to be what he ought to be, that is, honestly and naturally human. And this is neither so easy nor so impossible as one might think. At bottom, it consists in putting our acts and aspirations in accordance with the law of our being, and consequently with the Eternal Intention which willed that we should be at all.

—CHARLES WAGNER.
The Simple Life.

Wiser it were to welcome and make ours
Whate'er of good, though small, the Present brings,—
Kind greetings, sunshine, song of birds, and flowers,
With a child's pure delight in little things;
And of the griefs unborn to rest secure,
Knowing that Mercy ever will endure.

—RICHARD CHENEVIX TRENCH.
"To the Same." The Story of Justin Martyr.
Sabbation and Other Poems.

In character, in manner, in style, in all things, the supreme excellence is simplicity.

—HENRY WADSWORTH LONGFELLOW.

Small kindnesses, small courtesies, small considerations, habitually practiced, give a greater charm to the character than the display of great talents and accomplishments.

—MARY ANN KELTY.
The Value of Simplicity.

Occupy thyself with few things, says the philosopher, if thou wouldst be tranquil. The greatest part of what we say and do being unnecessary, if a man takes this away, he will have more leisure and less uneasiness. Accordingly, on every occasion a man should ask himself, is this one of the unnecessary things? Now a man should take away not only unnecessary acts, but also unnecessary thoughts, for thus superfluous acts will not follow after.

—MARCUS AURELIUS.
The Meditations of Marcus Aurelius.

Exactness in little duties is a wonderful source of cheerfulness.

—FREDERICK WILLIAM FABER.
Growth in Holiness; or, The Progress of the Spiritual Life.

This deliverance of the soul from all useless, and selfish, and unquiet cares, brings to it a peace and freedom that are unspeakable; this is true simplicity.

Simplicity consists in a just medium, in which we are neither too much excited, nor too sedate. The soul is not carried away by external things, so as to be unable to reflect; neither does it make those continual references to self, which a jealous sense of its own excellence multiplies to infinity. That freedom of the soul, which looks straight onward in its path, losing no time to reason upon its steps, to study them, or to dwell upon those which it has already taken, is true simplicity.

—FRANÇOIS DE SALIGNAC DE LA MOTHE FÉNELON.
Selections from Fénelon. Wisdom Series.

Act by not acting;
do by not doing.
Enjoy the plain and simple.
Find that greatness in the small.
Take care of difficult problems
while they are still easy;
Do easy things before they become too hard.
Difficult problems are best solved while they are easy.
Great projects are best started while they are small.
The Master never takes on more than she can handle,
which means that she leaves nothing undone.

—LAO TZU.
Tao Te Ching.

All the strength of the world and all its beauty, all true joy, everything that consoles, that feeds hope, or throws a ray of light along our dark paths, everything that makes us see across our poor lives a splendid goal and a boundless future, comes to us from people of simplicity, those who have made another object of their desires than the passing satisfaction of selfishness and vanity, and have understood that the art of living is to know how to give one's life.

—CHARLES WAGNER.
The Simple Life.

The spirit of simplicity is a great magician. It softens asperities, bridges chasms, draws together hands and hearts. The forms which it takes in the world are infinite in number;

but never does it seem to us more admirable than when it shows itself across the fatal barriers of position, interest, or prejudice, overcoming the greatest obstacles, permitting those whom everything seems to separate to understand one another, esteem one another, love one another.

—CHARLES WAGNER.
The Simple Life.

Little things come daily, hourly, within our reach, and they are not less calculated to set forward our growth in holiness, than are the greater occasions which occur but rarely.

Moreover, fidelity in trifles, and an earnest seeking to please God in little matters, is a test of real devotion and love.
Let your aim be to please our dear Lord perfectly in little things, and to attain a spirit of childlike simplicity and dependence.

—JEAN NICOLAS GROU.
The Hidden Life of the Soul.

.... to be in direct and personal contact with the sources of your material life; to want no extras, no shields; to find the universal elements enough; to find the air and the water exhilarating; to be refreshed by a morning walk or an evening saunter…to be thrilled by the stars at night; to be elated over a bird's nest or a wildflower in spring—these are some of the rewards of the simple life."

—JOHN BURROUGHS.
"An Outlook Upon Life." *Leaf and Tendril.*

Chapter 31

ON PATIENCE,
WAITING, FORBEARANCE

A noiseless patient spider,
I mark'd where on a little promontory it stood isolated,
Mark'd how to explore the vacant vast surrounding,
It launch'd forth filament, filament, filament, out of itself,
Ever unreeling them, ever tirelessly speeding them.

And you O my soul where you stand,
Surrounded, detached, in measureless oceans of space,
Ceaselessly musing, venturing, throwing, seeking the
spheres to connect them,
Till the bridge you will need be form'd, till the ductile
anchor hold,
Till the gossamer thread you fling catch somewhere, O
my soul.

—WALT WHITMAN.
"A Noiseless Patient Spider."

Patience is the guardian of faith, the preserver of peace, the
cherisher of love, the teacher of humility. Patience governs
the flesh, strengthens the spirit, stifles anger, extinguishes
envy, subdues pride; she bridles the tongue, refrains the

hand, tramples upon temptations, endures persecutions, consummates martyrdom. Patience produces unity in the church, loyalty in the state, harmony in families and societies; she comforts the poor and moderates the rich; she makes us humble in prosperity, cheerful in adversity, unmoved by calumny and reproach; she teaches us to forgive those who have injured us, and to be the first in asking forgiveness of those whom we have injured; she delights the faithful, and invites the unbelieving; she adorns the woman, and improves the man; is loved in a child, praised in a young man, admired in an old man; she is beautiful in either sex and every age.

—BISHOP GEORGE HORNE.
Prose Quotations from Socrates to Macaulay.

How poor are they who have not patience! What wound did ever heal but by degrees.

—WILLIAM SHAKESPEARE.
Othello. Act II, Scene iii.

Serene, I fold my hands and wait,
Nor care for wind, nor tide, nor sea;
I rave no more 'gainst time or fate,
For, lo! my own shall come to me.

I stay my haste, I make delays,
For what avails this eager pace?
I stand amid the eternal ways,
And what is mine shall know my face.

Asleep, awake, by night or day,
The friends I seek are seeking me;
No wind can drive my bark astray,
Nor change the tide of destiny.

What matter if I stand alone?
I wait with joy the coming years;
My heart shall reap where it hath sown,
And garner up its fruit of tears.

The waters know their own and draw
The brook that springs in yonder height;
So flows the good with equal law
Unto the soul of pure delight.

The stars come nightly to the sky;
The tidal wave unto the sea;
Nor time, nor space, nor deep, nor high,
Can keep my own away from me.

—JOHN BURROUGHS.
"Waiting."

In your patience possess ye your souls.

—LUKE 21:19. *KJV.*

Either teach them better if it be in thy power; or if it be not, remember that for this use, to bear with them patiently, was mildness and goodness granted unto thee.

—MARCUS AURELIUS.
The Meditations of Marcus Aurelius.

He that is slow to anger is better than the mighty; and he that ruleth his spirit than he that taketh a city

—PROVERBS 16:32. *KJV.*

It's a sign of a noble heart dowered with patience, never to be in a hurry, never to be in a passion. First be master over yourself if you would be master over others. You must pass through the circumference of time before arriving at the centre of opportunity. A wise reserve seasons the aims and matures the means. Time's crutch effects more than the iron club of Hercules. God Himself chasteneth not with a rod but with time. He spake a great word who said, "Time and I against any two." Fortune herself rewards waiting with the first prize.

—BALTASAR GRACIÁN.
The Art of Worldly Wisdom.

Be not hasty in thy spirit to be angry: for anger resteth in the bosom of fools.

—ECCLESIASTES 7:9. *KJV.*

Favorinus tells us how Epictetus would also say that there were two faults far graver and fouler than any others— inability to bear, and inability to forbear, when we neither patiently bear the blows that must be borne, nor abstain from the things and the pleasures we ought to abstain from.

"So," he went on, "if a man will only have these two words at heart, and heed them carefully by ruling and watching over himself, he will for the most part fall into no sin, and his life will be tranquil and serene." He meant the words Avexou kai apexou—"Bear and Forbear".

—EPICTETUS.
The Golden Sayings of Epictetus.

Endeavour to be patient in bearing with other men's faults and infirmities whatsoever they be, for thou thyself also hast many things which have need to be borne with by others. If thou canst not make thine own self what thou desireth, how shalt thou be able to fashion another to thine own liking. We are ready to see others made perfect, and yet we do not amend our own shortcomings.

—THOMAS À KEMPIS.
The Imitation of Christ.

Lord! who Thy thousand years dost wait
To work the thousandth part
Of Thy vast plan, for us create
With zeal a patient heart.

—JOHN HENRY NEWMAN.
"Zeal and Patience."
The Dream of Gerontius and Other Poems.

Take heed of despising "the day of small things," by looking after some great visitation, proportionable to thy distress, according to thy eye. Nay, thou must become a child; thou must lose thy own will quite by degrees. Thou must wait for life to be measured out by the Father, and be content with what proportion, and at what time, He shall please to measure.

—Isaac Penington.
Letters of Isaac Penington.

Waiting with me has been mainly a cheerful acquiescence in the order of the universe as I found it—a faith in the essential veracity of things. I have waited for the sun to rise and for the seasons to come; I have waited for a chance to put in my oar.

—John Burroughs.
"An Outlook Upon Life." *Leaf and Tendril.*

There is an adage, "In the ascent of a mountain, patience must be exercised on the steep hillside. In a journey along a snow-covered road, patience is also most needed in crossing dangerous bridges." Significant is the repetition of the word patience. The warning holds good to human affairs. When dealing with crafty and insidious men, or when journeying through the rough ways of life, the word must be our watchword; else how can we escape going astray into jungles or falling down into ditches?

—Hung Ying-Ming.
Musings of a Chinese Vegetarian.

But if we hope for that we see not, then do we with patience
wait for it.

—ROMANS 8:25. *KJV.*

To know how to separate things is to know how to enjoy
them. Many finish their fortune sooner than their life: they
run through pleasures without enjoying them, and would like
to go back when they find they have over-leaped the mark.
Postilions of life, they increase the ordinary pace of life by
the hurry of their own calling. They devour more in one day
than they can digest in a whole life-time; they live in advance
of pleasures, eat up the years beforehand, and by their hurry
get through everything too soon. Even in the search for
knowledge there should be moderation, lest we learn things
better left unknown. We have more days to live through than
pleasures. Be slow in enjoyment, quick at work, for men see
work ended with pleasure, pleasure ended with regret.

—BALTASAR GRACIÁN.
The Art of Worldly Wisdom.

Patience, though I have not
The thing that I require,
I must of force, God wot,
Forbear my most desire;
For no ways can I find
To sail against the wind.
Patience, do what they will
To work me woe or spite,

I shall content me still
To think both day and night,
To think and hold my peace,
Since there is no redress.

Patience of all my harm,
For fortune is my foe;
Patience must be the charm
To heal me of my woe:
Patience without offence
Is a painful patience.

—THOMAS WYATT.
"When Fortune Smiles Not, Only Patience Comforteth."

Patience is the finest and worthiest part of fortitude, and the rarest too…Patience lies at the root of all pleasures, as well as of all powers. Hope herself ceases to be happiness when Impatience companions her.

—JOHN RUSKIN.
The Works of John Ruskin.

Now to conclude; upon all occasion of sorrow remember henceforth to make use of this dogma, that whatsoever it is that hath happened unto thee, is in very deed no such thing of itself, as a misfortune; but that to bear it generously, is certainly great happiness.

—MARCUS AURELIUS.
The Meditations of Marcus Aurelius.

Chapter 32

ON HUMILITY, HUMBLENESS

Of all the causes which conspire to blind
Man's erring judgment and misguide the mind,
What the weak head with strongest bias rules,
Is pride, the never-failing vice of fools.

—ALEXANDER POPE.
An Essay on Criticism, Part 2.

Be not wise in thine own eyes.

—PROVERBS 3:7. *KJV.*

For whenever a man by proclaiming his good deeds receives the recompense of fame, he diminishes in a measure the secret reward of a good conscience.

—BOETHIUS.
The Consolation of Philosophy of Boethius.

Pride goeth before destruction, and an haughty spirit before a fall.

—Proverbs 16:18. *KJV.*

Don't be deceived by the crafty by putting too much confidence in them. Don't have too high an opinion of yourself, lest you should act with rashness. Don't disclose another's defect in order to display your own forte. Don't be envious of another's talent because of your own inferiority.

—Hung Ying-Ming.
Musings of a Chinese Vegetarian.

If you desire to know or learn anything to your advantage, then take delight in being unknown and unregarded.

A true understanding and humble estimate of oneself is the highest and most valuable of all lessons. To take no account of oneself, but always to think well and highly of others is the highest wisdom and perfection.

—Thomas à Kempis.
The Imitation of Christ.

Be humble if thou wouldst attain to Wisdom. Be humbler still, when Wisdom thou hast mastered.

—Helena Petrovna Blavatsky.
*The Voice of the Silence: And Other Chosen Fragments
from the Book of the Golden Precepts.*

I would not ask Thee that my days
Should flow quite smoothly on and on,
Lest I should learn to love the world
Too well, ere all my time was done.

But I would ask a humble heart,
A changeless will to work and wake,
A firm faith in Thy providence,
The rest—'tis thine to give or take.

—ALFRED NORRIS.
"A Prayer." *Inner and Outer Life: Poems.*

God resisteth the proud, but giveth grace unto the humble.

—JAMES 4:6. *KJV.*

The more humble and obedient to God a man is, the more wise and at peace he will be in all that he does.

—THOMAS À KEMPIS.
The Imitation of Christ.

Let another man praise thee, and not thine own mouth; a stranger, and not thine own lips.

—PROVERBS 27:2. *KJV.*

To be willing to be nothing.
To do the work, and erase the workman.
To paint the picture, and remove the palettes and myself.
To build a temple, and be willing to be the bearer of the
chalice, the keeper of the vestry, the swayer of the burning
myrrh.
To build me a lofty spire to the sky, not in pride but in all
humility. It shall touch the heavens, while I, its humble
builder, kneel lowly on its stone steps to pray.

—MURIEL STRODE.
"LXXI." *A Soul's Faring.*

A man's pride shall bring him low: but honour shall uphold
the humble in spirit.

—PROVERBS 29:23. *KJV.*

To resume and conclude, it is an error to think that our
advantages, whatever they are, should be put to the service
of our vanity. Each of them constitutes for him who enjoys
it an obligation and not a reason for vainglory. Material
wealth, power, knowledge, gifts of the heart and mind,
become so much cause for discord when they serve to
nourish pride. They remain beneficent only so long as they
are the source of modesty in those who possess them.

—CHARLES WAGNER.
The Simple Life.

Chapter 33

ON KINDNESS, COMPASSION, SYMPATHY

Who is thy Neighbor? – he who comes
To list the sufferer's heartfelt pains –
And hears, in feeble voice of one,
The cry of mankind's coarser strains –
Asks not if ill that grief atone,
Be direful guilt or folly's stains –
With heart of love, extends his hand to labor
For good and right of Man – He is thy Neighbor!

—HESTER S. Dwinelle.
"Who is thy Neighbor."

"Who is thy neighbor?". First, it is the sufferer, wherever, whoever, whatsoever he be. Wherever thou hearest the cry of distress; wherever thou seest any one struck down by the injustice, by the oppression, by the licentiousness, the selfishness of men; wherever thou seest any one brought across thy path by the chances and changes of life, that is, by the Providence of God, whom it is in thy power to help, - he, stranger or enemy though he be, - he is thy neighbor.

And, secondly, it is he that showed mercy. He, whosoever he be, that shows a sense of mercy, of justice, of self-control, of self-denial for the sake of others, he, little as thou mayest think it, he is thy neighbor.

—ARTHUR PENRHYN STANLEY.
"The Good Samaritan."

How many a knot of mystery and misunderstanding would be untied by one word spoken in simple and confiding truth of heart! How many a rough path would be made smooth, and crooked way, made straight! How many a solitary place would be made glad if love were there; and how many a dark dwelling would be filled with light!

—ORVILLE DEWEY.
Discourses on Human Life.

And be ye kind one to another.

—EPHESIANS 4:32. *KJV.*

Myself am a little universe. Let my passions be moderate and my likes and dislikes be well-regulated, and then my conduct will conform of itself to the laws of the universe, in which the elements are so harmoniously combined. Heaven and earth are the great parents of all creation. If a man acts so as not to provoke the complaint of his fellow-creatures and not to bring disaster on all, he will become a spirit of universal fellowship and benevolence.

—HUNG YING-MING.
Musings of a Chinese Vegetarian.

Since trifles make the sum of human things,
And half our mis'ry from our foibles springs;
Since life's best joys consist in peace and ease,
And few can save or serve, but all may please:
Oh! let th' ungentle spirit learn from hence,
A small unkindness is a great offence.

—HANNAH MOORE.
Sensibility: An Epistle to the Honourable Mrs. Boscawen.

A child's kiss
Set on thy singing lips shall make thee glad;
A poor man served by thee shall make thee rich;
A sick man helped by thee shall make thee strong;
Thou shalt be served thyself by every sense
Of service thou renderest.

—ELIZABETH BARRET BROWNING.
"Reward of Service."

As we have therefore opportunity, let us do good unto all men.

—Galatians 6:10. *KJV.*

Let the weakest, let the humblest in this congregation remember, that in his daily course he can, if he will, shed around him almost a heaven. Kindly words, sympathizing attentions, watchfulness against wounding men's sensitiveness,—these cost very little, but they are priceless in their value. Are they not, brethren, almost the staple of our daily happiness? From hour to hour, from moment to moment, we are supported, blest, by small kindnesses.

—Frederick William *Robertson.*
Sermons Preached at Trinity Chapel,
Brighton: Second Series, Volume 2.

Ask Him to increase your powers of sympathy: to give you more quickness and depth of sympathy, in little things as well as great. Opportunities of doing a kindness are often lost from mere want of thought. Half a dozen lines of kindness may bring sunshine into the whole day of some sick person. Think of the pleasure you might give to some one who is much shut up, and who has fewer pleasures than you have, by sharing with her some little comfort or enjoyment that you have learnt to look upon as a necessary of life, - the pleasant drive, the new book, flowers from the country, etc. Try to put yourself in another's place. Ask "What should I like myself, if I were hard-worked, or sick, or lonely?" Cultivate the habit of sympathy.

—GEORGE HOWARD WILKINSON.
Instructions in the Devotional Life.

Men, be kind to your fellow-men; this is your first duty, kind to every age and station, kind to all that is not foreign to humanity. What wisdom can you find that is greater than kindness?

—JEAN-JACQUES ROUSSEAU.
Emile. Book II.

Chapter 34

ON LIVING IN THE PRESENT MOMENT, THE ETERNAL NOW

No longer forward nor behind,
I look in hope or fear;
But grateful take the good I find,
The best of now and here.

—JOHN GREENLEAF WHITTIER.
"My Psalm."

This is the day which the LORD hath made; we will rejoice and be glad in it.

—PSALM 118:24. *KJV.*

How people will cry out against me! I hear from afar the shouts of that false wisdom which is ever dragging us onwards, counting the present as nothing, and pursuing without a pause a future which flies as we pursue, that false wisdom which removes us from our place and never brings us to any other.

—JEAN-JACQUES ROUSSEAU.
Emile. Book II.

The true felicity of life is to be free from perturbations; to understand our duties toward God and man; to enjoy the present without any anxious dependence upon the future. Not to amuse ourselves with either hopes or fears, but to rest satisfied with what we have, which is abundantly sufficient; for he that is so wants nothing. The great blessings of mankind are within us, and within our reach; but we shut our eyes and, like people in the dark, we fall foul upon the very thing we search for without finding it.

—Lucius Annaeus Seneca.
"Of A Happy Life."

These roses under my window make no reference to former roses or to better ones; they are for what they are; they exist with God to-day. There is no time to them. There is simply the rose; it is perfect in every moment of its existence. Before a leaf-bud has burst, its whole life acts; in the full-blown flower there is no more; in the leafless root there is no less. Its nature is satisfied, and it satisfies nature, in all moments alike. But man postpones or remembers; he does not live in the present, but with reverted eye laments the past, or, heedless of the riches that surround him, stands on tiptoe to foresee the future. He cannot be happy and strong until he too lives with nature in the present, above time.

—Ralph Waldo Emerson.
"Self-Reliance." *Essays, First Series.*

Time with his back against the mighty wall,
Which hides from view all future joy and sorrow,
Hears, without answer, the impatient call
Of puny man, to tell him of to-morrow.

Moral, be wise, and to the silence bow,
These useless and unquiet ways forsaking;
Concern thyself with the Eternal Now -
To-day hold all things, ready for thy taking.

—ELLA WHEELER WILCOX.
"The Eternal Now."

Take therefore no thought for the morrow: for the morrow shall take thought for the things of itself. Sufficient unto the day is the evil thereof.

—MATTHEW 6:34. *KJV.*

Listen to the Exhortation of the Dawn!
Look to this Day! For it is Life,
The very Life of Life.
In its brief course lie all the Varieties
And Realities of your Existence;
The Bliss of Growth,
The Glory of Action,
The Splendor of Beauty;
For Yesterday is but a Dream,
And Tomorrow is only a Vision;
But Today well lived

Makes every Yesterday a Dream of Happiness,
And every Tomorrow a Vision of Hope.
Look well therefore to this Day!
Such is the Salutation of the Dawn.

—Kalidasa.
"Salutation to the Dawn."

They do me wrong who say I come no more
When once I knock and fail to find you in;
For every day I stand outside your door
And bid you wake, and rise to fight and win.
Wail not for precious chances passed away!
Weep not for golden ages on the wane!
Each night I burn the records of the day—
At sunrise every soul is born again!

—Walter Malone.
"Opportunity."

The robbers of time are the past and the future. Man should bless the past, and forget it, if it keeps him in bondage, and bless the future, knowing it has in store for him endless joys, but live fully in the now.

—Florence Scovel Shinn.
The Game of Life and How to Play It.

Would'st shape a noble life? Then cast
No backward glances toward the past,
And though somewhat be lost and gone,
Yet do thou act as one new-born;
What each day needs, that shalt thou ask,
Each day will set its proper tasks.

—JOHANN WOLFGANG VON GOETHE.
Zahme Xenien, Vierte Abtheilung.

Let us then think only of the present, and not even permit our minds to wander with curiosity into the future. This future is not yet ours; perhaps it never will be. It is exposing ourselves to temptation to wish to anticipate God, and to prepare ourselves for things which He may not destine for us. If such things should come to pass, He will give us light and strength according to the need. Why should we desire to meet difficulties prematurely, when we have neither strength nor light as yet provided for them? Let us give heed to the present, whose duties are pressing; it is fidelity to the present which prepares us for fidelity in the future.

—FRANCOIS DE LA MOTHE FÉNELON.
Selections from Fénelon.

Happy the Man, and happy he alone,
He, who can call to day his own:
He who, secure within, can say,
To morrow do thy worst, for I have liv'd to-day.
Be fair, or foul, or rain, or shine,
The joys I have possest, in spight of fate, are mine.
Not Heav'n it self upon the past has pow'r;
But what has been, has been, and I have had my hour.

—JOHN DRYDEN.
"The Twenty-ninth Ode of the Third Book of Horace."

Happy he,
Self-centred, who each night can say,
"My life is lived: the morn may see
A clouded or a sunny day:
That rests with Jove: but what is gone,
He will not, cannot turn to nought;
Nor cancel, as a thing undone,
What once the flying hour has brought.

—HORACE.
"Odes 3.29." *The Odes and Carmen Saeculare of Horace.*

Happy men are full of the present, for its bounty suffices them; and wise men also, for its duties engage them. Our grand business undoubtedly is, not to see what lies dimly at a distance, but to *do* what lies clearly at hand.

Know'st thou Yesterday, its aim and reason;
Work'st thou well Today, for worthy things?
Calmly wait the Morrow's hidden season,
Need'st not fear what hap soe'er it brings.

But man's "large discourse of reason" will look "before and after"; and, impatient of the "ignorant present time," will indulge in anticipation far more than profits him. Seldom can the unhappy be persuaded that the evil of the day is sufficient for it; and the ambitious will not be content with present splendour, but paints yet more glorious triumphs, on the cloud-curtain of the future.

—Thomas Carlyle.
"Signs of the Times."

Trust no Future, howe'er pleasant!
Let the dead Past bury its dead!
Act,—act in the living Present!
Heart within, and God o'erhead!

—Henry Wadsworth Longfellow.
"A Psalm of Life."

Out of that care for the morrow which our Lord denounces, spring the fever of speculation, the hasting to be rich, endless scheming, continual reactions of fantastic hope and deep depression in individuals, of mad prosperity and intense suffering in nations.

If we had prayed for this day's bread, and left the next to itself, if we had not huddled our days together, not allotting to each its appointed task, but ever deferring that to the future, and drawing upon the future for its own troubles, which must be met when they come whether we have anticipated them or not, we should have found a simplicity and honesty in our lives, a capacity for work, an enjoyment in it, to which we are now, for the most part, strangers.

—FREDERICK DENISON MAURICE.
The Prayer Book.

The shadow by my finger cast
Divides the future from the past:
Before it, sleeps the unborn hour
In darkness, and beyond thy power:
Behind its unreturning line,
The vanished hour, no longer thine:
One hour alone is in thy hands,—
The NOW on which the shadow stands.

—HENRY VAN DYKE.
"The Sun-Dial at Wells College."

We live not in our moments or our years—
The Present we fling from us like the rind
Of some sweet Future, which we after find
Bitter to taste, or bind that in with fears,
And water it beforehand with our tears –
Vain tears for that which never may arrive:
Meanwhile the joy whereby we ought to live,
Neglected or unheeded, disappears.
Wiser it were to welcome and make ours
Whate'er of good, though small, the Present brings,—
Kind greetings, sunshine, song of birds, and flowers,
With a child's pure delight in little things;
And of the griefs unborn to rest secure,
Knowing that Mercy ever will endure.

—RICHARD CHENEVIX TRENCH.
"To the Same." *The Story of Justin Martyr. Sabbation and
Other Poems.*

Chapter 35

ON SUCCESSFUL LIVING, LIVING WITH PURPOSE

He has achieved success who has lived well, laughed often, and loved much; who has gained the respect of intelligent men and the love of little children; who has filled his niche and accomplished his task, whether by an improved poppy, a perfect poem, or a rescued soul; who has never lacked appreciation of Earth's beauty or failed to express it; who has always looked for the best in others and given them the best he had; whose life was an inspiration and whose memory a benediction.

—BESSIE ANDERSON STANLEY.
"What is Success?"

Lives of great men all remind us
We can make our lives sublime,
And, departing, leave behind us
Footprints on the sands of time;

Footprints, that perhaps another,
Sailing o'er life's solemn main,
A forlorn and shipwrecked brother,
Seeing, shall take heart again.

Let us, then, be up and doing,
With a heart for any fate;
Still achieving, still pursuing,
Learn to labor and to wait.

—Henry Wadsworth Longfellow.
"A Psalm of Life."

To live content with small means; to seek elegance rather than luxury, and refinement rather than fashion: to be worthy, not respectable; and wealthy, not rich; to study hard, think quietly, talk gently, act frankly; to have an oratory in my own heart, and present spotless sacrifices of dignified kindness in the temple of humanity; to spread no opinions glaringly out like show-plants, and yet leave the garden gate ever open for the chosen friend and the chance acquaintance: to make no pretenses to greatness; to seek no notoriety; to attempt no wide influence; to have no ambitious projects; to let my writings be the daily bubbling spring flowing through constancy, swelled by experiences, into the full, deep river of wisdom; to listen to stars and buds, to babes and sages, with open heart; to bear all cheerfully, do all bravely, await occasions, hurry never;… in a word, to let the spiritual, unbidden and unconscious, grow up through the common. This is to be my symphony.

—William Henry Channing.
"My Symphony."

For what is a man profited, if he shall gain the whole world, and lose his own soul?

—MATTHEW 16:26. *KJV.*

Love all, trust a few. Do wrong to none.

—WILLIAM SHAKESPEARE.
All's Well That Ends Well. Act 1 Scene 1.

Let me but live my life from year to year,
With forward face and unreluctant soul;
Not hurrying to, nor turning from the goal;
Not mourning for the things that disappear
In the dim past, nor holding back in fear
From what the future veils; but with a whole
And happy heart, that pays its toll
To Youth and Age, and travels on with cheer.

So let the way wind up the hill or down,
O›er rough or smooth, the journey will be joy:
Still seeking what I sought when but a boy,
New friendship, high adventure, and a crown,
My heart will keep the courage of the quest,
And hope the road›s last turn will be the best.

—HENRY VAN DYKE.
"Life."

Did you ever hear of a man who had striven all his life faithfully and singly toward an object and in no measure obtained it? If a man constantly aspires, is he not elevated? Did ever a man try heroism, magnanimity, truth, sincerity, and find that there was no advantage in them, – that it was a vain endeavor?

—HENRY DAVID THOREAU.
"Letter: 27 March (1848): Henry David Thoreau to Harrison Blake." *The Writings of Henry David Thoreau.*

The pleasures of youth may excel in keenness and in zest, but they have at the best a tinge of anxiety and unrest; they cannot have the fulness and depth which may accompany the consolations of age, and are amongst the richest rewards of an unselfish life.

For as with the close of the day, so with that of life; there may be clouds, and yet if the horizon is clear, the evening may be beautiful.

—SIR JOHN LUBBOCK.
"The Destiny of Man." *The Pleasures of Life.*

Lead a good life. Two things bring life speedily to an end: folly and immorality. Some lose their life because they have not the intelligence to keep it, others because they have not the will. Just as virtue is its own reward, so is vice its own punishment. He who lives a fast life runs through life in a double sense. A virtuous life never dies. The firmness of the soul is communicated to the body, and a good life is long not only in intention but also in extension.

—BALTASAR GRACIAN.
The Art of Worldly Wisdom.

Life 's more than breath and the quick round of blood;
It is a great spirit and a busy heart.
The coward and the small in soul scarce do live.
One generous feeling—one great thought—one deed
Of good, ere night, would make life longer seem
Than if each year might number a thousand days,
Spent as is this by nations of mankind.
We live in deeds, not years; in thoughts, not breaths;
In feelings, not in figures on a dial.
We should count time by heart-throbs. He most lives
Who thinks most—feels the noblest—acts the best.

—PHILIP JAMES BAILEY.
"Scene V, A Country Town." *Festus, a Poem.*

But by dint of action, and exacting from himself strict account of his deeds, man arrives at a better knowledge of life. Its law appears to him, and the law is this: Work out your mission. He who applies himself to aught else than the realization of this end, loses in living the raison d'etre of life. The egoist does so, the pleasure-seeker, the ambitious: he consumes existence as one eating the full corn in the blade, he prevents it from bearing its fruit; his life is lost. Whoever, on the contrary, makes his life serve a good higher than itself, saves it in giving it. Moral precepts, which to a superficial view appear arbitrary, and seem made to spoil our zest for life, have really but one object - to preserve us from the evil of having lived in vain. That is why they are constantly leading us back into the same paths; that is why they all have the same meaning: Do not waste your life, make it bear fruit; learn how to give it, in order that it may not consume itself! Herein is summed up the experience of humanity, and this experience, which each man must remake for himself, is more precious in proportion as it costs more dear.

—CHARLES WAGNER.
The Simple Life.

Use all your hidden forces. Do not miss
The purpose of this life, and do not wait
For circumstance to mould or change your fate.
In your own self lies Destiny. Let this
Vast truth cast out all fear, all prejudice,
All hesitation. Know that you are great,
Great with divinity. So dominate
Environment, and enter into bliss.

—ELLA WHEELER WILCOX.
"Attainment."

REFERENCES

Al-Ghazzali, Mohammed. *The Alchemy of Happiness.* Translated from the Hindustani by Claud Field. John Murray, Albemarle Street, W., 1910.

Allen, James. *As A Man Thinketh.* 1903.

Armstrong, John. "Book IV." *The Art of Preserving Health: A Poem.* A. Millar, 1944.

Arnold, Edwin. *The Light of Asia: Or, The Great Renunciation.* Roberts Brothers, 1880.

Arnold, Matthew. "Empedocles on Etna. Act I. Scene I." *Empedocles on Etna, and Other Poems.* B. Fellowes, 1852.

Aurelius, Marcus. *The Meditations of Marcus Aurelius.* Translated by George Long. Blackie & Son Ltd., 1910.

Bacon, Francis. "Of Fortune." *Essays or Counsels Civil and Moral. The Works of Francis Bacon.* C. and J. Rivington [etc.], 1826.

Bailey, Philip James. "Scene V, A Country Town." *Festus, a Poem.* B. B. Mussey, 1847.

Basford, James Lendall. *Sparks from the Philosopher's Stone.* David Bogue, 1882.

Bennett, Arnold. *How to Live on Twenty-four Hours a Day.* George H. Doran Company, 1910.

Besant, Annie. *The Meaning and Method of the Spiritual Life.* Theosophical Publishing House, 1911.

---. "Some Difficulties of the Inner Life." *Some Problems of Life.* Theosophical Publishing Society, 1900.

The Bhagavad-Gita (From The Mahabharata). Translated from the Sanskrit Text by Sir Edwin Arnold. Truslove, Hanson & Comba, Ltd., 1900.

Blake, William. "Auguries of Innocence."

---. "Eternity."

Blavatsky, Helena Petrovna. *The Voice of the Silence: And Other Chosen Fragments from the Book of the Golden Precepts.* Aryan Theosophical Press, 1909.

Boethius. *The Consolation of Philosophy.* Translated by Henry Rosher James. Edition used: *King Alfred's Version of the Consolations of Boethius.* Done into Modern English, with an Introduction by Walter John Sedgefield. Clarendon Press, 1900.

---. *The Consolation of Philosophy.* Translated by W. V. Cooper. J.M. Dent and Company, 1902.

---. *The Consolation of Philosophy of Boethius.* Translated into English Prose and Verse by H.R. James. Elliot Stock,1897.

"Brihadâranyaka Upanishad IV.4.5." *The Upanishads.* Translated by Max Muller, Vol II. From *Sacred Books of the East, Volumes 15.* 1884.

Brontë, Charlotte. "Life." *Poems by Currer, Ellis, and Acton Bell.* Aylott and Jones, 1846.

Browning, Elizabeth Barrett. "Reward of Service."

Browning, Robert. "Rabbi Ben Ezra." *Dramatis Personae.* Chapman and Hall, 1864.

Bryant, William Cullen. "Thanatopsis."

---. "To A Waterfowl."

Burroughs, John. "The Divine Soil." *Leaf and Tendril.* Houghton, Mifflin and Company, 1908.

---. "An Outlook Upon Life."

---. "Waiting." *The Little Book of American Poets: 1787-1900.* Editor Jessie B. Rittenhouse. Riverside Press, 1915.

Burton, Robert. *The Anatomy of Melancholy...Being an Abridgment of Burton's Celebrated Work.* N. Hailes, 1824.

Byron, George Gordon (Lord Byron). *The Island, or Christian and His Comrades.* John Hunt, 1923.

Carlyle, Thomas. "Characteristics." *The Edinburgh Review.* Edinburgh, Vol. LIV. December, 1831.

---. "Chapter 11: Labour." *Past and Present.* 1843.

---. *On Heroes, Hero-worship and the Heroic in History.* From *Thomas Carlyle's Collected Works.* Chapman and Hall, 1840.

---. *Sartor Resartus (1831) Lectures on Heroes (1840).* Chapman and Hall, 1864.

---. "Signs of the Times." *The Collected Works of Thomas Carlyle.* Chapman and Hall, 1858.

---. "Today."

Carruth, William Herbert. "Each in His Own Tongue." *The Little Book of American Poets.* Edited by Jessie B. Rittenhouse. Houghton Mifflin Company, 1915.

Channing, William Henry. "My Symphony." In *Memoir of William Henry Channing* by Octavius Brooks Frothingham. Houghton, Mifflin, 1886.

Cheney, John Vance. "Thanks." *Poems.* Houghton, Mifflin and Company, 1905.

---. "The Music of Nature."

Chuang Tzu. *Chuang Tzu Mystic, Moralist, and Social Reformer.* Translated from the Chinese by Herbert A. Giles. Bernard Quaritch, 1889.

Cicero, Marcus Tullius. "Book V. Whether Virtue Alone Be Sufficient for A Happy Life." *Cicero's Tusculan Disputations.* Literally translated, chiefly by Charles Duke Yonge. Harper & Brothers. 1877.

---. *De Senectute (On Old Age).* Translated with an Introduction and Notes by Andrew P. Peabody. Little, Brown, and Company, 1887.

Clarke, James Freeman. "The Education of Courage." *Self-culture: Physical, Intellectual, Moral, and Spiritual: A Course of Lectures.* James R. Osgood and Company, 1881.

Cotter, Joseph S., Jr. "Rain Music." *The Book of American Negro Poetry.* Edited by James Weldon Johnson. Harcourt, Brace and Company, 1922.

Cotton, Charles. "Contentment. Pindarick Ode." *Poems on Several Occasions.* Tho. Basset, and Will. Hinsman and Tho. Fox, 1689.

---. "Contentment. Pindaric Ode." *Poems on Several Occasions.* From *The Works of the English Poets from Chaucer to Cowper. Volume 6.* Edited by Samuel Johnson. J. Johnson, 1810.

Cotton, Nathaniel. "The Fire-Side." *The Works of the British Poets. Volume Eleventh.* By John Anderson. John and Arthur Arch, 1795.

Cowper, William. "Exhortation to Prayer." *The Poetical Works of William Cowper.* Edited by Eva Hope. Walter Scott, 1885.

---. "Ode to Peace."

---. "The Fable." *The Works of William Cowper: His Life, Letters, and Poems.* Edited by Thomas Shuttleworth Grimshawe. Phillips, Sampson, and Company, 1855.

Cranch, Christopher Pearse. "Gnosis." *Gems of Genius in Poetry and Art.* Edited by Frederick Saunders, Minnie K. Davis. Thompson & Thomas, 1899.

Davies, John. "The Immortality of the Soul." *Select Poetry: Chiefly Devotional, of the Reign of Queen Elizabeth, Part 1.* Edited by Edward Farr. University Press, 1845.

Da Vinci, Leonardo. *The Literary Works of Leonardo Da Vinci.* Compiled and edited from the Original Manuscripts by Jean Paul Richter. Samson Low, Marston, Searle and Rivington, 1883.

---. *The Notebooks of Leonardo Da Vinci.* By Jean Paul Richter. 1883.

De Sales (St), Francis. *A Selection from the Spiritual Letters of s. Francis de Sales.* Translated by Henrietta Louisa Lear. Rivingtons, 1880.

Dewey, Orville. *Discourses on Human Life*. David Felt, 1841.

The Dhammapada. Translated from the Pali by F. Max Muller. Volume X of *The Sacred Books of the East*. Oxford, the Clarendon Press, 1881.

Dogen Zenji. "Genjo Koan."

Donne, John. "Meditation XVII. Devotions Upon Emergent Occasions." *The Works of John Donne. Volume 3*. Edited by Henry Alford. John W. Parker, 1839

Dryden, John. "The Twenty-ninth Ode of the Third Book of Horace." *The Poems of John Dryden*. Edited by John Sargeaunt. Oxford University Press, 1913.

Dunbar, Paul Laurence. "A Choice."

---. "A Poet and His Song".

---. "A Thanksgiving Poem."

Dwinelle, Hester S. "Who is thy Neighbor." *Poems*. Claudian Press, 1900.

Ehrmann, Max. "Desiderata."

Eliot, George (Mary Ann Evans). *The Mill on the Floss*. 1867.

Emerson, Ralph Waldo. "Ali Ben Abu Taleb." *Poems/ Translations*.

---. *The Divinity School Address*.

---. *Essays, First Series*.

    ---. "Circles."

    ---. "Compensation."

    ---. "History."

---. "The Over-Soul."

---. "Self-Reliance."

---. "Spiritual Laws."

---. *Essays, Second Series.*

---. "Experience."

---. "New England Reformers."

---. "Fate." *The Conduct of Life.*

---. *Parnassus. An Anthology of Poetry.*

---. *Poems.*

---. "Fragments on Nature and Life. Nature."

---. "Woodnotes I."

---. "Terminus."

---. "Voluntaries." *May-day, and Other Pieces.*

Epictetus. *All the Works of Epictetus, which are Now Extant: Consisting of His Discourses, Preserved by Arrian, in Four Books, the Enchiridion, and Fragments, Volume 2.* Translated by Elizabeth Carter. J. and F. Rivington, 1768.

---. *Epictetus: The Discourses and Manual, Together With Fragments of His Writings.* Translated by P E Matheson. The Clarendon Press, 1916.

---. *The Golden Sayings of Epictetus. With the Hymn of Cleanthes.* Translated and Arranged by Hastings Crossley. Macmillan, 1912.

---. *The Works of Epictetus: Consisting of His Discourses, in Four Books, the Enchiridion, and Fragments.* A translation from the Greek based on that of Elizabeth Carter, by Thomas Wentworth Higginson.

Epicurus. *Letter to Menoeceus.* Translated by Robert Drew Hicks.

Faber, Frederick William. *Growth in Holiness; or, The Progress of the Spiritual Life.* John Murphy and Company, 1855.

---. *Spiritual conferences.* Edition 2. T. Richardson, 1860.

Fénelon, Francois de Salignac de La Mothe. *A Demonstration of the Existence and Attributes of God.* William Gillmor, 1811.

---. *Selections from Fénelon. Wisdom Series.* Roberts Bros., 1879.

---. *Spiritual Progress.* M. W. Dodd, 1853.

Fitzgerald, Edward. "Chronomoros." *Letters and Literary Remains of Edward FitzGerald. Volume III.* Edited by William Aldis Wright. Macmillan and Company, 1889.

Franklin, Benjamin. "To Josiah Franklin." (Letter to his father, 1738.) *The Works of Benjamin Franklin. Volume 7.* Edited by Jared Sparks. Whittemore, Niles, and Hall, 1856.

---. *Poor Richard's Almanack.*

Gibran, Kahlil. *The Prophet.* Alfred A Knopf, 1923.

Gladstone, William Ewart. *The Vatican Decrees in Their Bearing on Civil Allegiance.* 1874.

Goethe, Johann Wolfgang Von. *The Maxims and Reflections of Goethe.* Translated by Baily Saunders. The Macmillan Company. 1906.

---. *Torquato Tasso.* From *Beautiful Thoughts from German and Spanish Authors.* Compiled by Craufurd Tait Ramage Edward Howell. 1868.

---. *Zahme Xenien, Vierte Abtheilung.* From Thomas Huxley's "Universities: Actual and Ideal". *Science and Culture, and Other Essays.* Poem translation credit to Thomas Huxley's wife, Henrietta.

Goldsmith, Oliver. "The Deserted Village." *The Poems of Oliver Goldsmith.* Edited by Robert Aris Willmott. George Routledge and Sons, 1877.

Gracián, Baltasar. *The Art of Worldly Wisdom.* Translated by Joseph Jacobs. Macmillan and Company, 1892.

Granville, George (Lord Lansdowne). Epistle to Mrs. Elizabeth Higgons, 1690. "Occasioned by the Foregoing Verses. Written in the year 1690." *Poems of George Granville, Lord Lansdowne* in *The Works of the English Poets, from Chaucer to Cowper: Volume 11.* Edited by Alexander Chalmers. J. Johnson, 1810.

Gray, Thomas. "Ode on the Pleasure Arising from Vicissitude."

Greaves, James Pierrepont. From *The Unity of Truth. A Devotional Diary, Compiled from the Scriptures and Other Sources.* By Mary Ann Kelty. Trubner and Company, 1867.

Grou, Pere Jean Nicolas. *The Hidden Life of the Soul [By J.N. Grou].* From the Fr. by the Author of a Dominican Artist. Translated by Henrietta Louisa Lear. 1870.

Guyon. Madame. *A Short Method of Prayer and Spiritual Torrents.* Translated by A. W. Marston. Sampson Low, Marston, Low, & Searle, 1875.

Hall, E.B. *Thoughts*. Compiled by Jessie K. Freeman, Sarah S. B. Yule. Dodge Publishing Company, 1901.

Hall, Robert. *The Works of the Rev. Robert Hall, Volume 2.* G. & C. & H. Carvill, 1830.

Harper, Frances Ellen Watkins. "A Grain of Sand."

Hazlitt, William. "CCLXXXVII." *Characteristics: in the manner of Rochefoucault's Maxims*. Edited by Richard Henry Horne. J. Templeman, 1837.

---. "On Poetry in General." *Lectures on the English Poets. Delivered at the Surrey Institution*. Taylor and Hessey, 1818.

Henley, William Ernest. "Invictus."

Henry, James. "Luck." *Poems, Chiefly Philosophical*. C. C. Meinhold and Sons, 1856.

Herbert, George. "Gratefulness." *Parnassus: An Anthology of Poetry*. Edited by Ralph Waldo Emerson. Houghton, Osgood, and Company, 1880.

Holmes, Oliver Wendell, Sr. "The Chambered Nautilus."

---. "Contentment."

Horace (Quintus Horatius Flaccus). "Hor. Ep. xi. lib. I." Elphinston translation. "No. 6." *The Rambler.*

---. "Ode 4.10." *The Odes*. Philip Francis translation. From Samuel Johnson. "No. 38." *The Rambler.*

---. *The Odes and Carmen Saeculare of Horace*. Translation by John Conington. George Bell and Sons, 1882.

   ---. "Odes 2.10."

---. "Odes 3.29."

---. "Odes 4.7."

Horne, Bishop George. From *Prose Quotations from Socrates to Macaulay*. Compiled by S. Austin Allibone. J. B. Lippincott & Co., 1880.

Horton, George Moses. "Departing Summer."

Hume, David. "Essay 15: The Epicurean." *Essays Moral, Political, and Literary, Volume 1*. Edited by Thomas Hill Green, Thomas Hodge Grose. Longmans, Green, and Company, 1875.

---. "Essay 16: The Stoic."

Hung Ying-Ming. *Musings of a Chinese Vegetarian*. Translated by Yaichiro Isobe. Yuhodo, Kanda. 1926.

Huxley, Thomas Henry. *Aphorisms and Reflections*. Selected by Henrietta A. Huxley. Macmillan and Co. Limited, 1907.

Issa, Kobayashi. "The World of Dew."

James, William. *The Varieties of Religious Experience*. Longmans, Green, and Co., 1902.

Johnson, James Weldon. "Prayer at Sunrise." *Fifty Years & Other Poems*. Cornhill Company, 1917.

Johnson, Samuel. *"No. 6." The Rambler*.

---. *"No. 17." The Rambler*.

---. *"No. 38." The Rambler*.

---. *The Wisdom of the Rambler, Adventurer, and Idler*. Longman, Brown, Green and Longmans, 1848.

---. *The Works of Samuel Johnson, LL.D., in Nine Volumes, Volume the Second.*

Kabir. *Songs of Kabir.* Translated by Rabindranath Tagore. The Macmillan Company, 1915.

Kalidasa. "Salutation to the Dawn." (Author unknown. From the Sanskrit; also attributed to Kalidasa).

Keats, John. "Ode (Bards of Passion and of Mirth)." *The Poems of John Keats.* Edited by E. De Selincourt. Dodd, Mead and Company, 1905.

Keble, John. "Morning." *The Christian Year.* Cassell & Company, Limited, 1887.

---. "St. Matthew." *The Edinburgh Christian Magazine.* Paton and Ritchie, 1852.

Kelty, Mary Ann. *The Value of Simplicity.* Edited by Mary Minerva Barrows. H.M. Caldwell Co., 1905.

Kempis, Thomas À. *The Imitation of Christ.* Translation by William Benham. P. F. Collier & Son, 1909-14.

Khayyam, Omar. *Rubaiyat of Omar Khayyam.* Rendered into English Verse by Edward Fitzgerald.

Kilmer, Joyce. "Trees."

Lao Tzu. *Tao Te Ching* by Lao-Tzu. Complete online text, a translation for the public domain by J. H. McDonald, 1996.

Law, William. *The Works of the Reverend William Law, M.A.in Nine Volumes. Volume VI.* J. Richardson, 1792. Edition reprint by G. Moreton, 1893.

Le Galliene, Richard. "Inscriptions." *English Poems*. John Lane, 1895.

---. "Time Flies."

Lessing, Gotthold Ephraim. *Minna von Barnhelm or Soldier's Fortune*. Translated by Otto Heller. Henry Holt and Company, 1917.

Li Bai. "The Ching-ting Mountain." *The Works of Li Po, the Chinese Poet*. Translated by Shigeyoshi Obata. E.P. Dutton & Company, 1922.

Longfellow, Henry Wadsworth. "The Day is Done."

---. "A Psalm of Life."

---. "The Rainy Day."

---. "Retribution."

---. "The Village Blacksmith."

Loveman, Robert. "April Rain."

Lowell, James Russell. *The Vision of Sir Launfal and Other Poems*. Charles E. Merrill Company.

Lubbock, John. *The Pleasures of Life: Part I and Part II*. Macmillan, 1891.

---. "The Beauties of Nature."

---. "The Destiny of Man."

---. "The Duty of Happiness."

---. "Labor and Rest."

---. "The Value of Time."

Maeterlinck, Maurice. *Wisdom and Destiny.* Translated by Alfred Sutro. Dodd, Mead, and Company, 1900.

"Majjhima-Nikaya ii.32." *The Middle-length Discourses of the Buddha.*

Malone, Walter. "Opportunity." *The Little Book of American Poets: 1787-1900.* Edited by Jessie B. Rittenhouse. Riverside Press, 1915.

Manning, Henry Edward. *Sermons. Volume the Second.* Stanford and Swords, 1848.

---. *Sermons, Volume the Fourth.* William Pickering, 1850.

Martineau, James. *Endeavors after the Christian Life.* American Unitarian Association, 1881.

---. *Hours of Thought on Sacred Things. Volume 1.* Longmans, Green, Reader and Dyer, 1876.

Matsuo, Bashō.

Maurice, Frederick Denison. *The Prayer Book.* Macmillan, 1880.

Milton, John. From *The World's Laconics: Or The Best Thoughts of the Best Authors.* By Everard Berkeley (pseudonym of Tryon Edwards). M. W. Dodd, 1853.

Moore, Hannah. *Sensibility: An Epistle to the Honourable Mrs. Boscawen.* Meigs, Bowen, and Dana, 1785.

"Mundaka Upanishad I.1.6-7." *The Upanishads.* Translated by Max Muller. Vol II. From *Sacred Books of the East, Volumes 15.*

Newman, John Henry. "Zeal and Patience." *The Dream of Gerontius and Other Poems.* H. Milford, 1914.

---. "Zeal and Patience." *Verses on Various Occasions.* Burns, Oates, and Company, 1880.

Norris, Alfred. "A Prayer." *Inner and Outer Life: Poems.* Henry S. King and Co., 1875.

Noyes, Alfred. "The Loom of Years." *Collected Poems, Volume 1.* Frederick A. Stokes Company, 1913.

Olser, William. *Aequanimitas.* P. Blakiston's Sons and Company, 1904.

---. *A Way of Life.* Constable and Company Ltd., 1913.

Osgood, Frances S. "Golden Rules in Rhymes." *Poems.* Clark & Austin, 1848.

Ovid (Publius Ovidius Naso). *Metamorphoses, XV.* Samuel Johnson's *Rambler, No. 102.* Translation by James Elphinston.

---. *Metamorphoses, XV.* Translated by Sir Samuel Garth, John Dryden, Alexander Pope, Joseph Addison, William Congreve and other eminent hands.

Panchadasi. *The Spirit of the Upanishads (or the Aphorisms of the Wise).* Yogi Publication Society, 1907.

P'ang Yün (aka Layman P'ang).

Parker, Theodore. "Traits and Illustrations of Human Character and Conduct." *The Collected Works of Theodore Parker: Volume XIV. Lessons from the World of Matter and the World of Man.* Trübner and Company, 1872.

Pascal, Blaise. *Pensées (Thoughts.)* Translated by William Finlayson Trotter. P.F. Collier & Son Company, 1909-14.

Penington, Isaac. *Letters of Isaac Penington*. Nathan Kite, 1842.

Plutarch. "On Contentedness of Mind." *Plutarch's Morals: Ethical Essays*. Translated with Notes and Index by Arthur Richard Shilleto. George Bell and Sons, 1898.

Poile, M. Frances. "Silence." *Mental Chemistry*. Charles Francis Haanel. 1922.

Pope, Alexander. *An Essay On Man. Moral Essays and Satires*. Cassell & Company, Limited. 1891.

---. *Pope's Essay on Man, and Essay on Criticism*. Editor: Joseph Bartlett Seabury. Silver, Burdett, 1900.

---. "Universal Prayer."

Procter, Adelaide Anne. "Give." *Legends and Lyrics: A Book of Verses*. D. Appleton and Company, 1858.

Pusey, Edward Bouverie. *Parochial Sermons, Volume 2*. James Parker & Co., 1868.

Rabelais, Francois. *Gargantua. The Works of Francis Rabelais, Volume 1*. Translated by Thomas Urquhart and Peter Anthony Motteux. H. G. Bohn, 1854.

Robertson, Frederick William. *Sermons Preached at Trinity Chapel, Brighton: Second Series, Volume 2*. Ticknor and Fields, 1858.

Rousseau, Jean-Jacques. *Emile, or Education*. Translated by Barbara Foxley. Dent, 1911.

Royce, Josiah. *The Spirit of Modern Philosophy; An Essay in the Form of Lectures*. Houghton Mifflin Company, 1892.

Ruskin, John. "The Eagle's Nest." *The Works of John Ruskin*. George Allen, 1880.

Santayana, George. "O World." *Library of the World's Best Literature, Ancient and Modern, Volume 28*. Edited by Charles Dudley Warner, Hamilton Wright Mabie, Lucia Isabella Gilbert Runkle, George Henry Warner. J. A. Hill & company, 1902.

Scott, Walter. "Canto VI. Stanza 17." *Marmion*.

Seneca, Lucius Annaeus. "Of a Happy Life." *Minor Dialogues: Together with the Dialogue on Clemency*. Translated by Aubrey Stewart. George Bell and Sons, 1889.

---. *Moral letters to Lucilius. Volume 2. (Seneca Ad Lucilium Epistulae Morales)*. Translated by Richard Mott Gummere. William Heinemann and G.P. Putnam's Sons.

   ---. "Epistle LXXVIII. On the Healing Power of the Mind."

   ---. "Epistle LXXXVII. Some Arguments in Favour of the Simple Life."

---. "Of a Happy Life." *Seneca's Morals by Way of Abstract*. By Sir Roger L'Estrange. Jacob Tonson, 1718.

---. *On the Shortness of Life*. Translated by John W. Basore. William Heinemann, 1932.

Shakespeare, William. *All's Well That Ends Well*. Act 1, Scene 1.

---. *Hamlet*.

---. *Henry VI*. Part 3.

---. *A Midsummer Night's Dream*. Act 5, Scene 1.

---. *Othello.* Act II, Scene iii.

---. *Richard II.* Act 5, Scene 5.

---. "Sonnet XII."

Shelley, Percy Bysshe. "Love's Philosophy."

---. "Mutability."

---. "To a Skylark."

Shinn, Florence Scovel. *The Game of Life and How to Play It.* 1925.

Southey, Robert. *The Doctor, &c: In Two Volumes.* Harper & Brothers, 1836.

The Speaker's Garland. Volume 9. Edited by Phineas Garrett. The Penn Publishing Company, 1897.

Spinoza, Benedict de. *The Ethics (Ethica Ordine Geometrico Demonstrata).* Translated by R. H. M. Elwes.

The Spirit of the Upanishads: Or, The Aphorisms of the Wise. Volume 1. Yogi Publication Society, 1907.

Stanley, Arthur Penrhyn. "The Good Samaritan." *Unity of Evangelical and Apostolical Teaching: Sermons Preached Mostly in Canterbury Cathedral.* John Murray, 1859.

Stanley, Bessie Anderson. "What is Success?" *Heart Throbs, Volume Two.* Edited by Joe Mitchell Chapple. Chapple Publishing Company, 1911.

Strode, Muriel. *A Soul's Faring.* Boni and Liveright. 1921.

Sylvester, Joshua. "A Contented Mind." *The Fireside Encyclopaedia of Poetry.* Compiled and edited by Henry T. Coates. Porter & Coates, 1878.

Tao Te Ching by Lao-Tzu, Complete online text, a translation for the public domain by J. H. McDonald. 1996.

Taylor, Jeremy. *The Rules and Exercises of Holy Living.*

Temple, Anna. "The Kneeling Camel." *The Kneeling Camel and Other Poems.* Moffat, Yard & Company, 1920.

Thayer, William Roscoe. "Envoi." *Poems: New and Old.* Houghton Mifflin and Company, 1894.

Thomson, James. "Canto I." *Castle of Indolence. An Allegorical Poem.* A. Millar, 1748.

Thoreau, Henry David. *Walden.*

---. *The Writings of Henry David Thoreau: With Bibliographical Introductions and Full Indexes. In Ten Volumes, Volume 4.* Houghton, Mifflin, 1895.

---. *The Writings of Henry David Thoreau: Journal, Volume 8: 1854.*

Tolstoy, Leo. *War and Peace.*

Traherne, Thomas. *Centuries of Meditations.* Christian Classics Ethereal Library, 1908.

Trench, Richard Chenevix. "Century of Couplets." *Sabbation; Honor Neale; and Other Poems.* Edward Moxon, 1838.

---. "Some Murmur, When Their Sky is Clear."

---. "To the Same." *The Story of Justin Martyr: Sabbation and Other Poems.* Ed. Moxon, 1844.

Trine, Ralph Waldo. *In Tune with the Infinite.* Dodd, Mead & Company, 1897.

---. *This Mystical Life of Ours: A Book of Suggestive Thoughts for Each Week Through the Year Selected from the Works of Ralph Waldo Trine.* Thomas Y. Crowell & Company, 1907.

Tu Fu. "To Li Po on a Spring Day." *The Works of Li Po, the Chinese Poet.* Translated by Shigeyoshi Obata. E.P. Dutton & Company, 1922.

Van Dyke, Henry. "God of the Open Air." *Music and Other Poems.* C. Scribner's Sons, 1908.

---. "Katrina's Sun-Dial."

---. "Life."

---. "The Sun-Dial at Wells College."

---. "Work."

---. "Thoughts Are Things." *Mental Chemistry.* Charles Francis Haanel. 1922.

Vaux, Thomas (Thomas, Lord Vaux). "Of a Contented Spirit." *Chaucer to Burns, Volume 1 of English Verse.* Edited by W. J. Linton and R. H. Stoddard. Charles Scribner's Sons, 1883.

Voltaire (François-Marie Arouet). *Candide.* Boni and Liveright, Inc., 1918.

Von Goethe, Johann Wolfgang. *The Maxims and Reflections of Goethe.* Translated by Bailey Saunders. The Macmillan Company, 1906.

Wagner, Charles. *The Simple Life.* Translated from the French by Mary Louise Hendee. McClure, Phillips & Company, 1904.

Wesley, Charles. "Waiting for Christ the Prophet." *Hymns and Sacred Poems*, by John Wesley and Charles Wesley, The Second Edition. Felix Farley, 1715.

Wheatley, Phillis. "On Virtue." *Poems on Various Subjects, Religious and Moral*. W. H. Lawrence & Company, 1887.

Whitehead, William. ". On Nobility." *The Works of the British Poets with Prefaces, Biographical and Critical. Volume Eleventh*. By Robert Anderson. John & Arthur Arch, 1795.

Whitman, Walt. "A Noiseless Patient Spider." *Leaves of Grass. Volume 2 of The Complete Writings of Walt Whitman*. G. P. Putnam's Sons, 1902.

Whittier, John Greenleaf. "The Call of the Christian." *The Complete Poetical Works of John Greenleaf Whittier*. James R. Osgood and Company, 1876

---. "My Psalm."

---. "A Song of Harvest."

---. "To——, with a Copy of Woolman's Journal."

Wilkinson, George Howard. *Instructions in the Devotional Life*. 1877.

Wilcox, Elizabeth Wheeler. "Attainment." *Poems of Optimism*. Gay and Hancock, Ltd., 1903.

    ---. "Thanksgiving."

---. "The Eternal Now." *Poems of Optimism*. Gay and Hancock, Ltd., 1919.

    ---. "The Winds of Fate."

---. "Morning Prayer."

---. "Thanksgiving."

Wooton, Henry. "The Character of a Happy Life." *Reliquiæ Wottonianæ.* T. Roycroft, 1672.

Wordsworth, William. "The Rainbow."

Wyatt, Thomas. "When Fortune Smiles Not, Only Patience Comforteth." *Volume 2 of The Works of Henry Howard: Earl of Surrey and of Sir Thomas Wyatt the Elder.* Edited by Geo. Fred. Nott. Longman, Hurst, Rees, Orme, and Brown, 1816.

Young, Edward. *Night-Thoughts on Life, Death, and Immortality.* Chapman & Company, 1802.

Made in the USA
Columbia, SC
05 April 2021